YO-BZL-766

CANCELLED, DELAYED, GROUNDED

CECIL C. KUHNE III

CANCELLED, DELAYED, GROUNDED

LAW FOR THE FRUSTRATED AIR TRAVELER

Cover design by Kelly Book /ABA Publishing.

The materials contained herein represent the opinions of the authors and/or the editors, and should not be construed to be the views or opinions of the law firms or companies with whom such persons are in partnership with, associated with, or employed by, nor of the American Bar Association or the Section of Public Utility, Communications and Transportation Law unless adopted pursuant to the bylaws of the Association.

Nothing contained in this book is to be considered as the rendering of legal advice for specific cases, and readers are responsible for obtaining such advice from their own legal counsel. This book is intended for educational and informational purposes only.

Printed in the United States of America.

19 18 17 16 15   5 4 3 2 1

Library of Congress Cataloging-in-Publication Data

Kuhne, Cecil C., III, 1952- author.
  Cancelled, delayed, grounded : law for the frustrated air traveler / Cecil C. Kuhne III, American Bar Association.
    pages cm
  Includes bibliographical references and index.
  ISBN 978-1-62722-780-3 (softcover : alk. paper) -- ISBN 978-1-62722-781-0 (e-book) 1. Aeronautics, Commercial--Law and legislation--United States. 2. Aircraft occupants--Legal status, laws, etc.--United States. 3. Aeronautics, Commercial--Passenger traffic--Law and legislation--United States. 4. Consumer protection--Law and legislation--United States. I. American Bar Association. Solo, Small Firm and General Practice Division, sponsoring body. II. Title.
  KF2441.K84 2014
  343.7309'78--dc23   2014034829

Discounts are available for books ordered in bulk. Special consideration is given to state bars, CLE programs, and other bar-related organizations. Inquire at Book Publishing, ABA Publishing, American Bar Association, 321 N. Clark Street, Chicago, Illinois 60654-7598.

www.ShopABA.org

CONTENTS

INTRODUCTION — IX

CHAPTER 1 — 1
NADER'S RAIDERS

CHAPTER 2 — 7
THE WEDDING PARTY

CHAPTER 3 — 11
TRAPPED ON THE TARMAC

CHAPTER 4 — 17
AIRLINE DEREGULATION

CHAPTER 5 — 23
PASSENGER PARANOIA

CHAPTER 6 — 29
NEAR COLLISION

CHAPTER 7 — 33
CASH STASH

CHAPTER 8 — 41
BOARDING DENIED

CHAPTER 9 — 45
GUNS ON BOARD

CHAPTER 10 — 49
A LITTLE OUT OF HAND

CHAPTER 11 — 53
DEPLANED!

CHAPTER 12 — 61
FINAL JOURNEY

CHAPTER 13 — 63
STOLEN TICKETS

CHAPTER 14
HIJACKED!
67

CHAPTER 15
CRAMPED SEATS
71

CHAPTER 16
CLAIM CHECK
75

CHAPTER 17
PLANE CHANGE
79

CHAPTER 18
CHECKING CONTRABAND
83

CHAPTER 19
PRECIOUS CARGO
87

CHAPTER 20
FOOD AND WATER
91

CHAPTER 21
AGENT OF TRAVEL
95

CHAPTER 22
FREQUENT FLIERS
97

APPENDIX A
KNOW YOUR AIR TRAVEL RIGHTS
103

APPENDIX B
SHOT DOWN
119

APPENDIX C
ON STANDBY
133

APPENDIX D
RECONFIRMATION
141

APPENDIX E
OUTSIDE THE CONVENTION
147

APPENDIX F
ACCORD AND SATISFACTION
153

TIMELINE OF COMMERCIAL AVIATION
161

ABOUT THE AUTHOR
163

AIRLINES HAVE A STRICT POLICY OF NEVER REVEALING FLIGHT INFORMATION TO PASSENGERS. SAY YOU HAVE A TICKET FOR A FLIGHT THAT'S SCHEDULED TO DEPART AT 6 P.M. THE AIRPORT TV MONITORS WILL INSIST THAT THIS FLIGHT IS ON SCHEDULE, EVEN IF THE TIME IS 5:57 P.M. AND THERE IS NO ACTUAL, PHYSICAL AIRPLANE OUT AT THE END OF THE JETWAY. IF YOU ASK THE AIRLINE PERSONNEL ABOUT THIS, THEY'LL TAP ON THEIR COMPUTER KEYBOARD FOR A MOMENT, THEN LOOK YOU IN THE EYE AND SAY: "I'M STILL SHOWING THIS FLIGHT ON TIME."

+ + + + + + + + + + + + + + +

DAVE BARRY

INTRODUCTION

Consider the marvel that is modern air travel. According to the federal Bureau of Transportation Statistics, over 800 million passengers travel annually on airlines in the United States. Every year there are almost nine million departures (which works out to roughly 24,000 flights a day), and well over a billion revenue passenger miles. And this is just domestic travel. The bureau also keeps track of the various reasons for cancellations, delays, and groundings, the most common of which are foul weather, misconnected flights, air-traffic-control problems, and aircraft maintenance.

The magnitude of the undertaking is simply overwhelming. No wonder there are so many issues with the commercial aviation industry. Passengers, of course, do have legal and administrative rights (see Appendix A), as outlined in such statutes as the Federal Aviation Act, the Airline Deregulation Act, and the Warsaw Convention, and in those regulations promulgated by the Federal Aviation Agency and the Civil Aeronautics Board. Litigation, too, is always an option, and thus a number of the more intriguing cases are chronicled in the book before you.

Everyone you talk to, it seems, has an airline story. That may be because everyone has had an airline *experience*. Even a cursory review of reports from the newspapers reveals very unusual circumstances that can arise in this frantic-paced world of commercial aviation.

One of my favorite stories is that of the pilot for Pakistan International Airlines who threw a temper tantrum when he failed to receive his favorite breakfast. He refused to fly from New York to Lahore until he did. Employees of PIA were immediately dispatched to a local hotel to obtain this special meal (the contents of which were never revealed). As a result, the flight was delayed three hours.

I also enjoyed the story about the teacher from England who had flown to France to celebrate a school anniversary. Things went horribly wrong on the flight back, and what should have taken two hours turned into 30. The epic journey took this poor soul to six airports in three countries in two planes, not to mention two trips by motor coach and one by taxi. He could have easily flown to Australia in the time it took him to get home. The next time, the educator morosely remarked, he would just take the bus.

The worst stories, though, seem to come from the tarmac. A flight from Houston to Minneapolis was diverted to Rochester because of stormy weather, and it landed around midnight. Instead of allowing passengers to disembark and spend the night in the terminal, the airline decided to keep the passengers on board the aircraft. "It's not like you're on a 747 and can walk around," one passenger said. "This was a sardine can, with a single row of seats on one side of the plane and two rows of seats on the other. And you've got fifty people inside, including babies, for the whole night. It was a nightmare."

And then, of course, there's the inevitable passenger rage. Canadian police were called to the Calgary airport to calm a crowd of angry passengers following an 11-hour delay on a flight to Cancun, Mexico, during the Christmas holidays. Many of those waiting became unruly when they learned that the delays were due to flight attendants calling in sick. "There was literally almost a riot," one of the passengers reported. "There were people on chairs, screaming. It was not like anything I'd ever seen at an airport before."

A lot can happen here in the aviation domain, and contained in the book before you are just a few of the frustrating (and unfortunately all-too-familiar) circumstances associated with air travel that have, in turn, led to some fascinating litigation. At the boarding gate, for example, passengers are bumped, defamed by boarding agents, falsely accused of assaulting ground personnel, mistakenly informed that they can't bring on board their spouse's cremated remains (which are subsequently lost in checked luggage), and refused passage because their tickets were reported as stolen. In the air, there are hijackings with passengers taken hostage, preparations for crash landings before the engines suddenly re-engage, collisions with serving carts, falling luggage, allegedly rude and racist treatment by flight attendants, and even gunfire by Russian military aircraft. And if that weren't enough, you have the usual lost luggage (including mounds of cash), cocaine in an unidentified suitcase that is later claimed (along with the arrest of its owner), and seven thoroughbred dogs killed in transit by the stifling heat. And these are just a few of the stories included here.

Anyone who has traveled by plane has experienced these frustrations to some degree. But when you consider the sheer complexity of it all, it is remarkable how well the system *usually* works. So remember that the next time you're on a flight where everything has gone wrong and you feel like a helpless cow being herded down the highway on a cattle car. Don't get mad—just say *moo*.

1

+ + + + + + + + + + + + + + + + + + +

NADER'S RAIDERS
BUMPING AS FRAUDULENT MISREPRESENTATION

+ + + + + + + + + + + + + + + + + + +

NADER V. ALLEGHENY AIRLINES
626 F.2d 1031 (D.C. Cir. 1980)

Rarely does a lawsuit about airline overbooking reach the level of the U.S. Supreme Court, but then again, rarely does an airline bump a renowned consumer advocate like Ralph Nader. Along the way, the case became legendary among followers of the airline industry, and the D.C. Circuit Court of Appeals devoted two lengthy opinions to it.

The controversy first arose in April 1972 when Nader agreed to make several appearances in Connecticut to support the fundraising efforts of the Connecticut Citizen Action Group (CCAG). Nader was to speak at a noon rally in Hartford and then later at the campus of the University of Connecticut.

Three days earlier, Nader had reserved a seat on Allegheny Airlines Flight 864, which was scheduled to leave D.C. at 10:15 a.m. and arrive in Hartford at 11:15 a.m. Nader arrived at the gate five minutes before departure. He was told that all seats were taken, and that he, along with several others ahead of him, could not be accommodated. Explaining that he absolutely had to be in Hartford for the rally, Nader asked the agent to see if any standby passengers had been inadvertently allowed to board or if anyone would relinquish a seat.

Both requests were refused. Nader was offered alternative transportation by air taxi to Philadelphia, where connections could be made with an Allegheny flight scheduled to arrive in Hartford at 12:15. Concerned that the connection was too close, Nader rejected this option and chose instead to fly to Boston, where he was met by a CCAG staff member who drove him to the university.

Only two days before Nader made his reservation on Flight 864, he was bumped from an American Airlines flight. Six months before that, he had been bumped by Eastern Airlines on another flight. On both occasions he held a confirmed reservation. When the Allegheny ticket agent handed Nader the Denied Boarding Form required by Civil Aeronautics Board (CAB) regulations, he replied that he did not need it because "I already knew what it said."

Pursuant to CAB regulations, Allegheny mailed Nader a check in the whopping sum of $32.41 as denied boarding compensation. Nader's attorney promptly returned the check, together with a letter characterizing it as "wholly inadequate." (14 C.F.R. Part 250 now provides very clear rules for payment of denied boarding compensation to passengers and it was recently amended in 2011 to increase the sums payable to such passengers.)

THE LAWSUIT

In due course Nader sued Allegheny for compensatory and punitive damages. Well acquainted with the airline regulatory scheme, he did not seek compensation for the bumping per se, but asserted two other grounds of liability: (a) a common law action based on fraudulent misrepresentation arising from the airline's failure to inform him in advance of its deliberate overbooking practices, and (b) a statutory action based on the airline's failure to afford him the boarding priority specified in the rules filed with the CAB.

The district court entered a judgment for Nader, awarding him $10 in compensatory damages and $25,000 in punitive damages. However, the appellate court was unable to find any evidence of malice, and it reversed and remanded the case. The district court was instructed to stay further action pending referral to the CAB. In the interim, the U.S. Supreme Court concluded that the action could be heard by the trial court without action by the CAB.

On remand, the district court found that Allegheny violated section 404(b) of the Federal Aviation Act by its failure to accommodate Nader in accordance with its own priority boarding rules. For this, the court awarded him $10 in compensatory damages. The court also found that the airline's failure to notify Nader of the possibility of bumping constituted fraudulent misrepresentation, and that the airline "wantonly implemented its policy of nondisclosure and misrepresentation in conscious, deliberate, and callous disregard of the effect of its policy on its passengers." The court subsequently awarded Nader $15,000 in punitive damages.

Allegheny appealed the decision once again.

THE PRACTICE OF OVERBOOKING

Overbooking is a common practice in the airline industry, designed to ensure that each flight leaves with as few empty seats as possible despite a large number of "no-shows." Employing statistical studies of no-show patterns on specific flights, the airlines try to predict the appropriate number of reservations necessary to fill each flight. By doing this, they strive to ensure the most efficient use of aircraft while preserving a flexible booking system that permits passengers to cancel and change reservations freely. At times, of course, the practice of overbooking results in oversales, and when this occurs, some passengers are denied boarding. The chance that any particular passenger will be bumped is so negligible that even those aware of the possibility would hardly give it a second thought.

CAB regulations require each airline to establish priority rules for boarding passengers and to offer denied boarding compensation to bumped passengers. These liquidated damages are usually equal to the value of the passenger's ticket. Passengers are free to reject the compensation offered in favor of a common law suit for damages suffered as a result of the bumping. When it was initially promulgating its rule, the CAB rejected a proposal requiring explicit notice to passengers that they could be bumped even if they held confirmed seats. Instead, the Board promulgated a regulation that allowed overbooking to continue as long as carriers filed tariffs providing "prompt, effective and adequate compensation" to denied boarding passengers.

The CAB reasoned that were the carrier prevented from overbooking, large numbers of passengers would be denied reservations on flights which, due to no-shows, would depart with empty seats. A realistic view of overbooking leads to the conclusion that, even though it sometimes results in oversales, it contributes to flexibility and freedom in securing, changing, and cancelling reservations. Rigid controls over overbooking would inevitably reduce load factors, and the additional cost would ultimately be borne by the traveling public. Disclosure would only create anxiety and confusion among passengers, lead to a large number of duplicative and protective reservations, produce a rapid turnover in reservations within the 24 hours before the departure of a flight, and increase the no-show problem.

The appellate court reasoned that an airline may not therefore be condemned as a wanton wrongdoer for conforming to the standards set by the agency charged with the duty of regulating it. The award of punitive damages was accordingly set aside.

FRAUDULENT MISREPRESENTATION

The court turned to the question of whether Allegheny was guilty of fraudulent misrepresentation in failing to disclose to Nader that his "confirmed reservation" was subject to the contingency that he might be denied boarding if the flight was overbooked.

The record disclosed that in the 17 months preceding the Nader incident, Allegheny had experienced only *two* oversales on Flight 864, and statistical analyses confirmed there was only slightly more than one chance in 2,000 that a ticket holder would be denied boarding because of overbooking. Therefore, the odds that a holder of a confirmed reservation would be boarded were approximately 99.95 percent. Allegheny noted that the chance that Nader would be denied boarding was so remote as to be practically insignificant.

The airline reasoned that a confirmed reservation is not a guarantee, but rather a "reasonable assurance" of being flown, since any flight can be cancelled as the result of weather, mechanical problems, and the like. The airline argued that Nader had a reasonable assurance of being accommodated, and the chance of being bumped was too remote to affect that assurance. Silence about such a possibility, the airline contended, did not amount to a false representation of a material fact.

The district court agreed with Nader, concluding that confirmation of a reservation connoted a "guarantee" of flight subject only to contingencies beyond the control of the airline. The possibility of being bumped because of overbooking, the district court said, was a factor within the airline's control. In the view of the court, the fact that the possibility was slight did not make it any less material—it was still a factor in the equation.

The appellate court strongly disagreed. It held that Nader could not recover unless the evidence established that Allegheny intended to deceive him when it failed to notify him of its overbooking practice. The matter of overbooking, the court pointed out, had been thoroughly explored by the CAB in public hearings. In those proceedings, Allegheny had acknowledged its practice of overbooking and had explained its benefits. The record disclosed that the CAB's Office of Consumer Affairs had distributed 400,000 copies of a booklet on consumers' rights dealing with the subject of denied boarding. Overbooking had been discussed in periodicals of general circulation. The CAB had promulgated rules published in the Code of Federal Regulations. In short, the practice of overbooking was public knowledge.

In the light of these facts, the appellate court rejected the trial court's conclusion that Allegheny's failure to notify Nader about overbooking was motivated by deceit. Overbooking, the court said, was not a covert operation, and Allegheny was entitled to assume that passengers knew of the practice. Furthermore, Nader was a frequent traveler, an accomplished attorney, and a rigorous advocate of consumer rights, including those of airline passengers.

In other words, the evidence demonstrated that Nader was well aware that a confirmed reservation did *not* exclude the possibility that he might be bumped. The court sternly concluded that the irascible Mr. Nader was therefore entitled to neither compensatory nor punitive damages.

2

+ + + + + + + + + + + + + + + + + + + +

THE WEDDING PARTY
CLEARLY OVERBOOKED

+ + + + + + + + + + + + + + + + + + + +

SMITH V. PIEDMONT AVIATION
567 F.2d 290 (5th Cir. 1978)

All airlines are familiar with the predictable anger that sometimes erupts from a passenger who has been unceremoniously bumped. These feelings can become especially intense when a passenger has arrived at the gate hours before an overbooked flight and unknowingly watches a fellow passenger take his seat.

Three weeks before his departure in April 1974, Joseph Smith made a reservation on Piedmont Flight 944 from Atlanta to Bluefield, West Virginia. He was to be a groomsman in the wedding of a close friend in Tazewell, Virginia. His plans included the wedding rehearsal scheduled for 4:00 that afternoon and the rehearsal dinner that night. Smith was fastidious about his plans. He twice reconfirmed his reservation, and on the appointed day, he arrived at the boarding gate *two hours* ahead of scheduled departure.

When the flight was called for boarding, Smith did not immediately join the boarding line, because he (as it turned out) erroneously believed that his "confirmed" reservation guaranteed him a seat on the flight. Instead, he waited until the boarding line shortened before taking his place there. When Smith reached the counter he was informed that all available seats were filled and that he could not board the plane. Seven other reserved ticket holders were also denied boarding.

Two reasons were given by Piedmont for its inability to board those eight ticket holders. First, the plane was overweight because extra fuel had to be loaded in anticipation of bad weather. As a result, three seats had to be left empty to counterbalance the weight of the added fuel. Second, the flight had been overbooked by five.

After Smith was denied boarding, he requested that Piedmont remove his checked luggage since it contained his money. This request was refused. He next demanded that Piedmont arrange a charter flight to take him to Bluefield. He was told that this was impossible.

Piedmont did offer Smith alternate air travel to Bluefield, but he refused because the flights were full and he would have to fly standby. After Smith twice renewed his demand for a charter flight, the exasperated Piedmont agent finally blurted out, "I don't know when you're going to get it through your thick head we're not going to rent any airplanes or charter you a flight."

Smith finally selected an alternative flight from Atlanta to Roanoke, Virginia. After arriving in Roanoke, he rented a car and drove to Tazewell over unfamiliar mountain roads. He missed the wedding rehearsal, but did make it to part of the rehearsal dinner. In addition to providing this flight free of charge, Piedmont tendered Smith two checks. One, in the amount of $20, was a refund of the Roanoke to Bluefield fare. The other, for $43.18, was compensation for denied boarding. (Under the recently increased compensation rates for passengers denied boarding, Smith would have fared better.)

In his lawsuit, Smith presented evidence that Piedmont failed to follow its boarding priority rules filed with the Civil Aeronautics Board (CAB). These rules provided that in the event of an oversale situation, passengers in the same class were to be boarded according to the time and date of the booking of their reservation. However, Piedmont's agent boarded the flight on a first-come, first-served basis.

The boarding agent testified that his instructions were to consider the convenience of the passengers, to ensure that all passengers on board were confirmed, and, most important, to get the flight out on time. Compliance with the boarding priority rules would have substantially delayed the flight.

The district court awarded Smith compensatory damages in the precise amount of $1,051.80 and punitive damages in the sum of $1,500 for Piedmont's failure to comply with the Federal Aviation Act. On appeal, Piedmont argued that the finding of a violation of the act was not supported by the evidence. However, the court found that Piedmont's failure to follow its own boarding priority rules filed with the CAB undercut this argument. As for compensatory damages, Smith was admittedly due $63.18 for fare refund and denied-boarding compensation. This meant that Smith was awarded approximately $1,000 for inconvenience, inability to make the rehearsal on time, missing part of the rehearsal dinner, being required to drive an automobile on unfamiliar mountain roads, and the cost of a rental car.

In the appellate court's opinion, the compensatory award was generous but did not exceed the discretion allowed the trier of fact. Damage awards, the court reasoned, may not be overturned unless they shock the judicial conscience. The court found inadequate support in the record for the award of punitive damages. The court pointed out that mere inadvertence, or even gross negligence, is not sufficient to support an award of punitive damages. The tort must be aggravated by evil motive, actual malice, deliberate violence, or oppression.

The court noted that it was true that Piedmont failed to follow its boarding priority rules. In response to Smith's repeated demand that Piedmont charter a flight, the agent did refer to his "thick head," a reaction obviously provoked by Smith's boorish behavior. The court noted that such a rude remark might support an award of nominal damages, but the court was unable to discern evil motive, actual malice, deliberate violence, or oppression in the remark. The judgment for punitive damages was therefore reversed.

And the next time he arrives two hours early for a flight, the allegedly thick-headed Mr. Smith will no doubt check in the second he arrives.

3

+ + + + + + + + + + + + + + + + + + +

TRAPPED ON
THE TARMAC
A VERY LONG DAY

+ + + + + + + + + + + + + + + + + + +

RAY V. AMERICAN AIRLINES
609 F.3d 917 (8th Cir. 2010)

Catherine Ray and her husband boarded an American flight at 6:00 a.m. on December 29, 2006, traveling from Oakland to Dallas. Due to bad weather and a backup of flights in the Dallas area, the flight was diverted to Austin for refueling. The plane landed around noon, refueled, began to taxi toward the runway, and then stopped. At that point, the pilot informed the passengers that the Dallas airport was closed and that the plane could not take off until it reopened.

About an hour later, the pilot announced that a bus would be arriving to take any passengers who wished to deplane. Ray testified during her deposition that the pilot recommended that the passengers remain on board as it was likely they would be leaving within the next hour or so. She also testified that the pilot told passengers that if they chose to deplane, they would be "finished with this flight" and would be "on their own." The Rays assumed that the pilot meant that passengers would be required to find alternate transportation to Dallas, but they never asked for clarification. The Rays chose to remain on the plane when the bus arrived.

After two or three more hours, the pilot announced that a second bus would be coming to take any more passengers who wished to leave. Ray testified that when this bus arrived, the passengers were told, "This is your last chance, if you want to get off, get off now because this is it." The Rays again chose to remain on the plane.

For the next six to seven hours, American provided no further opportunities for passengers to leave the plane. Ray said the conditions on the plane deteriorated and the air became "stuffy" and "smelly." Passengers were only given "two or three granola bars" and "two soda pops." When Ray attempted to use one of the plane's lavatories, it would no longer flush, and there was no water to wash her hands. Ray said that at one point a passenger began arguing with a flight attendant and asked to see the pilot. When the pilot came out, the passenger demanded to be taken to a gate. Ray was concerned a fight would break out.

About 6:00 p.m., the pilot announced that he was no longer able to fly the plane because he had reached his maximum number of on-duty hours. He informed the passengers that he was trying to get the plane to a gate, but there was lightning in the area. At 9:00 p.m. the plane was moved to a gate, and the remaining passengers deplaned. Many of the passengers, including the Rays, spent the night in the terminal. (Regulations adopted by the Department of Transportation in 2011 now require airlines to develop tarmac delay contingency plans, including the provision of food, water, and working lavatories during any delays of more than two hours. These regulations also obligate carriers to return aircraft to the gate in the event of a delay of more than three hours for domestic flights and more than four hours for international flights. In October 2013, United Airlines was fined $1.1 million by the agency for 13 lengthy flight delays that occurred one stormy night at Chicago's O'Hare International Airport.)

The following morning American flew the Rays to Dallas, and they connected to another flight to Tulsa, Oklahoma. Ray testified that on the day after the delay, she experienced "some kind of intestinal stomach irritation," which she attributed to not being able to wash her hands on the plane.

Ray filed a putative class action against American, alleging state law claims for false imprisonment, negligence, intentional infliction of emotional distress, breach of contract, and fraud. She argued that the delay occurred because of American's "intentional or negligent lack of personnel, equipment, and planning for ordinary weather disruptions." She also claimed that American had decided for financial reasons not to allow passengers to deplane after the buses had left.

American moved to dismiss Ray's claims, contending they were preempted by the Federal Aviation Act (Aviation Act) and the Airline Deregulation Act (ADA). The district court granted the motion in part, concluding that (a) the Aviation Act precluded Ray from bringing state law claims based on the airline's decision to reroute the plane for safety reasons, and (b) the ADA preempted any state law claims seeking compensation for meals, lodging, ground transportation, and expenses during delays. Ray's breach of contract and fraud claims were also dismissed as preempted. The court concluded that the false imprisonment, emotional distress, and negligence claims were not preempted because they arose from American's actions after the flight was on the ground in Austin.

In October 2008, the district court filed its final scheduling order, and Ray filed a motion for class certification. American moved for summary judgment on Ray's remaining false imprisonment, emotional distress, and negligence claims, which the court granted. Ray appealed.

FALSE IMPRISONMENT

Under Texas law, the elements of a false imprisonment claim are: (1) willful detention, (2) without consent, and (3) without authority of law. The district court granted summary judgment to American after concluding that Ray could not prove that her detention on the plane was without consent and without authority of law. Ray claimed that she presented sufficient evidence to create issues of material fact on each of these elements.

Whether a plaintiff has consented to detention is ordinarily a question of fact for the jury unless the plaintiff has failed to present sufficient evidence for a reasonable jury to conclude that consent was lacking. Ray conceded that American offered passengers two opportunities to leave the plane by bus during the first several hours of the delay, and that she chose not to take either. At no point did she notify the flight crew that she wished to leave the plane. The district court concluded that these facts prevented Ray from satisfying the consent element of her false imprisonment claim.

On appeal, Ray presented a number of arguments challenging the court's conclusion with respect to consent. She asserted that (a) her consent was procured through deception, (b) she was not given a meaningful choice whether to deplane, (c) she was not required to vocalize her lack of consent, and (d) American exceeded the scope of her consent. The court felt that it need not reach these allegations because Ray failed to present sufficient evidence to show that her detention on American's plane was "without authority of law."

Under Texas law, the plaintiff bears the burden to prove the absence of authority in order to satisfy the final element of a false imprisonment claim. Ray did not present any statute or regulation that (a) placed a limit on the number of hours American was permitted to keep passengers aboard an aircraft during a delay, or (b) otherwise controlled the conduct Ray alleged formed the basis of her false imprisonment claim. Moreover, American did provide Ray with two opportunities to deplane, and the pilot informed the passengers that the second was their last chance to leave the flight.

Ray asserted that an airline lacked legal authority to keep a passenger on a plane if "exigent circumstances" required the passenger's release. The court concluded that Ray failed to present facts to show such circumstances existed in respect to her detention.

NEGLIGENCE

Ray argued that she presented sufficient evidence to create a genuine issue of material fact about whether American acted negligently by keeping passengers on the plane for hours, failing to provide enough food and beverages, allowing the lavatories to become dirty and in disrepair, and delivering passengers to the terminal after all airport restaurants had closed. To establish a claim for negligence under Texas law, a plaintiff must establish "a duty, a breach of that duty, and damages proximately caused by that breach." If a defendant violates a contractual obligation rather than a duty independently imposed by law, there can be no claim for negligence under Texas law. However, a contract between the parties may not supersede a claim for negligence if there is a special relationship between the parties.

The district court granted summary judgment to American after finding that the airline's "Conditions of Carriage" controlled the company's duties in the event of a lengthy onboard delay. American's conditions of carriage provide that:

> In the case of extraordinary events that result in very lengthy onboard delays, American will make every reasonable effort to ensure that essential needs of food (snack bar such as a Nutri-Grain), water, restroom facilities, and basic medical assistance are met. We are not responsible for any special, incidental, or consequential damages if we do not meet this commitment.

In the view of the appellate court, American's conditions of carriage document spelled out in sufficient detail the rights between the airline and its passengers. Alternatively, Ray argued that American, as a common carrier, owed her a duty above and beyond the conditions of carriage. Under Texas law, a common carrier owes its passengers "the high degree of care that a very cautious, prudent, and competent person would use under the same or similar circumstances." The court found that this duty would not be applicable here because Ray had presented no evidence that she suffered physical injury.

Under Texas law, a plaintiff must prove physical injury as a result of the defendant's negligent actions. During her deposition, Ray testified that she had felt mild claustrophobia while on the plane, but that moving to the window seat alleviated that sensation. She also testified that the next day she had an upset stomach which she attributed to not being able to wash her hands. However, she did not inform the flight crew about either situation, and she did not seek any medical treatment.

The judgment of the district court was therefore affirmed, leaving Mrs. Ray with little consolation for failing for refusing to take that first bus off the dreaded tarmac.

4

+ +

AIRLINE
DEREGULATION
A PREEMPTION DILEMMA

+ +

CHARAS V. TRANS WORLD AIRLINES
160 F.3d 1259 (9th Cir. 1999)

Over the years, the circumstances under which the federal Airline Deregulation Act (ADA) preempts state law claims have been the subject of much litigation, and some of the judicial results were clearly inconsistent. In a number of consolidated cases before the Ninth Circuit, the court sought to add some uniformity to its future decisions. The cases before the court involved a wide array of airline injuries:

- Robert Beverage claimed that a flight attendant slammed into his shoulder with a service cart, dislocating his shoulder and causing a cracked and detached scapular prosthesis (whatever that is, it must be painful).
- Mildred Jacoby alleged that after the plane landed, a passenger opened an overhead bin and a large piece of luggage fell squarely on her head.

- Cherie Charas awkwardly tripped over a piece of luggage left in the aisle by a flight attendant, resulting in a fractured humerus and requiring a shoulder joint replacement.
- Bernice Gulley had a serious medical condition that made her susceptible to bone fractures. She said she warned the airline of her condition and requested assistance in disembarking, but the airline was apparently unresponsive. Gulley exited the plane on a stairway with a single chain handhold, and she fell and injured herself.
- Elizabeth Newman claimed that when making her reservations, she informed the airline she was blind, had a heart condition, and required assistance in boarding the plane. She flew from Long Island to San Diego without incident. On her return, a flight attendant learned of her fragile condition and informed the captain. The airline then denied her passage until she could provide a letter from her doctor stating it was safe for her to fly. As a result, Newman's departure was delayed, and she had to spend the night at a hotel.

THE ADA STATUTE

At the time, Section 1305(a)(1) of the ADA provided:

> No State or political subdivision thereof . . . shall enact or enforce any law, rule, regulation, standard, or other provision having the force and effect of law relating to the rates, routes, or service of any air carrier [emphasis added].

The scope of this preemption has been a source of considerable dispute since its enactment. The Ninth Circuit eventually adopted the approach of the Fifth Circuit in *Hodges v. Delta Airlines, Inc.*, which held that claims related to a "service" provided by the airline *were* preempted by the ADA, but that claims related to an airline's "operations and maintenance" were *not*. In *Hodges*, an airline passenger was injured when a box containing several bottles of rum fell from an overhead bin and forcefully struck him.

The court in *Hodges* acknowledged that there is no strict dichotomy between "services" and "operation or maintenance of aircraft," and that the terms "overlap somewhat conceptually." The court ultimately concluded that the personal injury claim for the falling baggage was *not* related to the provision of airline services, but that it derived instead from the *operation* of the aircraft. Accordingly, the plaintiff's lawsuit was *not* preempted and could proceed apace.

Unfortunately, in future cases, the distinction between an airline's operations and its service turned out to be as elusive as it was unworkable. The service-versus-operations dichotomy produced nonsensical, inequitable, and inconsistent results, and most importantly, it had nothing to do with the purpose of airline deregulation. Thus, a plaintiff injured when struck by a beverage cart door would *not* be able to bring a tort action if the flight attendant negligently failed to latch the door properly (because the flight attendant's conduct related to "service"), but *would* be able to bring suit if the door swung open because a bolt was missing (on the theory that the injury arose out of the "operations and maintenance" of the aircraft).

SUPREME COURT PRECEDENT

Addressing the scope of the ADA, the U.S. Supreme Court had previously taken great pains to articulate the boundaries of the preemption, indicating that the ADA would not preempt most state law tort claims. In *Morales v. Trans World Airlines*, the Court faced the question of whether airlines were subject to states' laws banning deceptive advertising. The Court concluded that state restrictions on advertising were precisely the type of economic regulation that Congress intended to preempt in deregulating the airline industry. The Court therefore concluded that preemption prevented states from barring allegedly deceptive airline-fare advertisements through enforcement of their general consumer-protection statutes. The Court expressed its concern that, as an economic matter, state restrictions on fare advertising had a forbidden effect on fares.

The Court revisited the preemption issue in *American Airlines, Inc. v. Wolens*, determining that a state's consumer fraud statute could not be applied to American's decision to devalue mileage credits accrued by users of its frequent-flyer program. On the other hand, the Court held that a common law breach of contract suit by these program participants was not preempted because the claim simply sought to hold the parties to their agreements. Rather than involving "state-imposed obligations," these contracts involved "privately ordered obligations" and "self-imposed undertakings."

Wolens therefore indicated that preemption did not apply to all state law affecting the passenger-airline relationship. Even though the *Wolens* majority did not directly address whether common law torts were preempted, several justices did. Justice Stevens contended that "Congress did not intend to give airlines free rein to commit negligent acts subject only to the supervision of the Department of Transportation, any more than it meant to allow airlines to breach contracts with impunity."

In short, the Supreme Court strongly indicated that state tort law claims would not be barred. The Court thus explicitly limited its holding: "Some state actions may affect [airline fares] in too tenuous, remote, or peripheral a manner to have pre-emptive effect."

CONGRESSIONAL INTENT

The Ninth Circuit considered two presumptions about the nature of preemption. First, because the states are independent sovereigns in a federal system, it was presumed that Congress did not readily preempt state-law causes of action. Second, the analysis of the scope of the statute's preemption was guided by the Court's principle that congressional purpose is the ultimate touchstone in every preemption case. In all preemption cases, the court must start with the assumption that the historic police powers of the states were *not* to be superseded by the federal act unless that was the clear and manifest purpose of Congress.

It was evident to the Ninth Circuit that Congress's purpose in enacting the ADA was to achieve the economic deregulation of the airline industry and to promote "maximum reliance on competitive market forces." The purpose of preemption was to avoid state interference with federal deregulation. Nothing in the act itself, or its legislative history, indicated that Congress had a "clear and manifest purpose" to *displace* state tort law in actions that did not affect deregulation in more than a "peripheral manner." Furthermore, the fact that Congress did not intend the ADA to preempt all state tort claims was evident from at least two other provisions of the airline regulatory statutes.

First, airlines were still required to maintain insurance for death and bodily injury to passengers. Complete preemption of state law in the tort area would have rendered this requirement meaningless. Second, the savings clause, which provides that "nothing in this chapter shall in any way abridge or alter the remedies now existing at common law," evidenced congressional intent to prohibit states from regulating the airlines while preserving state tort remedies that already existed at common law, as long as such remedies did not significantly impact federal deregulation.

The court noted that airlines' "rates" and "routes" generally referred to the point-to-point transport of passengers. It therefore followed that "service" referred to such things as the frequency and scheduling of transportation, and to the selection of markets to which transportation is provided. To interpret "service" more broadly would ignore the context of its use and would result in the preemption of virtually everything an airline does. It seemed clear to the court that this is not what Congress intended. Nowhere in the legislative history did Congress intimate that "service" included the dispensing of food and drinks, flight attendant assistance, and the like.

The court therefore concluded that when Congress enacted deregulation of the airlines, it intended to insulate the industry from possible state economic regulation as well. It did not intend to immunize the airlines from liability for personal injuries caused by their tortious conduct. Like "rates" and "routes," Congress used "service" in the public utility sense, i.e., the provision of air transportation to and from various markets at various times. In that context, "service" did not refer to the pushing of beverage carts, keeping the aisles clear, the safe handling and storage of luggage, assistance to passengers in need, and so forth. Accordingly, the Ninth Circuit remanded the cases to the panel for a resolution consistent with its decision.

At long last, those airline passengers whose knees were unmercifully bashed by errant beverage carts had a reason to celebrate.

5

+ + + + + + + + + + + + + + + + + + + +

PASSENGER PARANOIA
A FIRST-CLASS ACT

+ + + + + + + + + + + + + + + + + + + +

FARASH V. CONTINENTAL AIRLINES, INC.
574 F.Supp.2d 356 (S.D.N.Y. 2008)

On January 5, 2006, Daniel Farash boarded Continental Airlines Flight 539, which departed from Miami for Newark. He had a first-class ticket, redeemed with frequent flyer miles, and he was assigned an aisle seat. Much to his delight, he saw that his seat was located in the bulkhead, and that the adjacent window seat was vacant. Seconds before the aircraft was to take off, the flight attendant (the court calls her "Jane Doe") allegedly "demanded" that Farash move to a nearby window seat so that a father traveling with his child could be accommodated.

Farash explained to Jane Doe that he suffered from psychological disorders that necessitated he sit in an aisle seat. Ms. Doe apparently ignored his objections and, according to Farash, treated him like a "farm animal or illegal trespasser." Farash moved to his new first-class seat, which he described as "a bastardized, claustrophobic window seat that did not recline nor have proper leg room." This caused Farash to feel "swindled, cheated, and disgusted." He found his new seat to be "qualitatively inferior to most other seats on the entire plane."

Farash said the trip was allegedly made all the more unpleasant because Ms. Doe harassed him and gave him inferior service, while the other passengers were treated "like royalty." Farash also claimed that he was "profiled and the subject of discrimination for being a single male, having Semitic looks and a middle-eastern last name."

It got worse. As Farash was leaving the lavatory, Jane Doe, "in a vindictive and appalling act of provocation," extended her legs out into the aisle to completely block his passage. Fearful of confronting her, Farash was "reduced to scaling the wall to avoid conflict." He then noticed that his original seat was being occupied by an adult, rather than a child. He summoned Ms. Doe and asked why he had been transferred from his original seat given that no child was sitting there. Farash said that Ms. Doe angrily shouted that the child was back in coach and then "stormed away."

Farash alleged that after moving into his new seat, he learned that the person seated next to him was a federal air marshal. Shortly after Farash asked Jane Doe why he had been transferred from his seat, Jane Doe summoned the air marshal to the front of the cabin. She motioned towards Farash while speaking to the air marshal, who then made eye contact with Farash for several seconds. Returning to his seat, the air marshal took out a "black book and searched through it." Farash alleged that these interactions with the air marshal "terrified, traumatized, and overwhelmed" him; that he had to maintain his composure to avoid a panic attack, as he was now certain that Jane Doe would go to any extreme to abuse him; and that he was "very anxious" that the air marshal would ground the plane and that he would be arrested and subjected to attention by the national news media.

When the flight landed in Newark, Ms. Doe supposedly ordered Farash to exit the plane in front of the air marshal. The next day, Farash called Continental Airlines to report the incident. The airline eventually informed him that after a full investigation his complaint was validated and that Jane Doe had broken company policy. Farash said he was put in contact with Allen Babbs, a Continental employee, who was "rude, insulting, unsympathetic, insensitive, and devious, treating customers as if they were on trial." After an interview, Mr. Babbs sent a letter stating that Continental assumed no responsibility in the matter.

Farash claimed that, as a result of his treatment by the airline, he has experienced emotional distress, insomnia, illness, a "breakdown," and a reoccurrence of post-traumatic stress disorder. He alleged that he was unable to concentrate and work effectively, resulting in monetary losses worth hundreds of thousands of dollars. He claimed that as a result he required "copious amounts of psycho-pharmaceutical medications" and developed hypertension, mood swings, and phobias. Farash sued the airline for negligence, gross negligence, and civil assault, and sought punitive damages. Continental moved to dismiss the complaint.

PREEMPTION UNDER THE AIRLINE DEREGULATION ACT

Continental argued that the entire complaint was preempted by the ADA and must be dismissed. To assess whether a tort claim should be preempted, the court applied the three-part test articulated in *Rombom v. United Air Lines, Inc.* Under this test, the court must first determine whether the activity at issue in the claim is an airline service. If so, then the court must decide whether the claim affects the airline service directly or tenuously, remotely, or peripherally. Finally, the court must decide whether the underlying tortious conduct was reasonably necessary to the provision of the service. If the tortious act did not occur during the service, or did not further the provision of service in a reasonable manner, then the state tort claim should continue.

CLAIMS FOR SEAT REASSIGNMENT

Farash first alleged that the flight attendant requested he move to another first-class seat. These claims, the court said, were all related to the efforts to resolve seat conflicts, and thus were clearly airline services. This set of claims also satisfied the second prong of the *Rombom* analysis because the claim affected the airline service directly. Turning to the third prong, the court concluded that the underlying conduct was reasonably necessary to the provision of the airline service of seating and reseating passengers.

In his complaint Farash stated that he felt that his reseating was the result of being "profiled and the subject of discrimination for being a single male, having Semitic looks and a middle eastern last name." The court held that this allegation could be construed as an argument that the flight attendant's motive in reseating plaintiff was *discriminatory*. A discriminatory reseating, the court said, is *not* reasonably necessary to the provision of an airline service, and indeed, federal law prohibits air carriers from discriminating on the basis of national origin and sex. Accordingly, plaintiff's claims based on his allegedly discriminatory seat reassignment were *not* preempted under the ADA.

CLAIMS FOR INTERACTIONS WITH THE AIR MARSHAL

The court found that the actions of the flight attendant in regard to the air marshal were airline services for the purposes of the ADA. The claims involving the air marshal met the second prong of the *Rombom* analysis because the claims directly affected the airline service. Turning to the third prong, the court had to determine whether these interactions were reasonably necessary to the provision of the service of in-flight security. Farash claimed that the flight attendant's motive was to harm him, and that the flight attendant acted out of discriminatory intent. The court concluded that such a discrimination claim cannot be preempted.

CLAIMS FOR IN-FLIGHT SERVICES

Farash made numerous allegations about the quality of the service on his flight and the conduct of the flight attendant, and the court held that all of these areas related to the services provided by an air carrier. Accordingly, the claims based on the quality of in-flight services and the conduct of the flight attendant were preempted under the ADA.

CLAIMS FOR POST-FLIGHT CUSTOMER SERVICE

Finally, Farash asserted that his claims related to Continental's post-flight customer service. Farash's principal objection to the customer service seemed to be that Continental Airlines did not give him the result he desired. But the court held that neither rudeness nor a refusal to give the customer sought-for relief constitute unreasonableness in the customer service department. As a result, the plaintiff's claims were preempted under the ADA.

FAILURE TO STATE A TORT CLAIM

To the extent that his action was not preempted by the ADA, the court held that Farash had nevertheless failed to state a cognizable claim under New York law. Indeed, the court found Farash's claims to be "patently frivolous."

NEGLIGENCE

Under New York law, a plaintiff must establish three elements to prevail on a negligence claim: (1) the existence of a duty on defendant's part as to plaintiff, (2) a breach of this duty, and (3) injury to the plaintiff as a result thereof.

Although Continental owed a duty of care to the plaintiff, this duty was not so broad as to protect plaintiff from the injuries he alleged. The court held that Farash's complaint essentially alleged that Continental owed him a heightened standard of care, rather than a reasonable one. Continental had no duty to provide plaintiff with the stress-free flight he demanded, to provide him with a higher standard of accommodations and service because he had a first-class seat, or to provide him with customer service that would bend to his whims.

GROSS NEGLIGENCE

To prevail on a claim for gross negligence, a plaintiff must also prove that defendant's conduct "evinces a reckless disregard for the rights of others or `smacks' of intentional wrongdoing." Because Farash had failed to make out a claim for ordinary negligence, his claim for gross negligence necessarily failed. The court said that the allegations set forth in the complaint came "nowhere close" to establishing the recklessness or intentional wrongdoing required under the fourth element of gross negligence.

CIVIL ASSAULT

Finally, Farash brought a claim for civil assault. Under New York law, a civil assault action lies where there is "an intentional attempt or threat to do physical injury or commit a battery," thereby placing an individual in reasonable apprehension of bodily harm. Farash failed to allege that the actions of the flight attendant or the air marshal placed him in *reasonable* apprehension of bodily harm. At most, Farash alleged that the flight attendant spoke with the air marshal and made a gesture toward him, and that the air marshal subsequently looked directly at him. These gestures, the court said, were insufficient as a matter of law to make out a claim for civil assault.

Similarly, plaintiff's allegation that the flight attendant extended her legs out into the aisle to block plaintiff's passage likewise failed to constitute civil assault. Farash conceded that he was not impeded by the flight attendant's conduct, and he did not allege any facts to suggest that this constituted an intentional or threatened attempt to do physical injury. Accordingly, the court dismissed Farash's claim of civil assault.

In the end, the court dismissed all of the plaintiff's complaint for the atrocities that allegedly occurred in first class. Those who fly coach might suggest that Mr. Farash join the rest of us in the back of the plane, where such treatment has come to be expected.

6

+ + + + + + + + + + + + + + + + + + + +

NEAR COLLISION
RECOVERING FOR
MENTAL ANGUISH

+ + + + + + + + + + + + + + + + + + + +

EASTERN AIRLINES V. FLOYD
499 U.S. 530 (1991)

On May 5, 1983, an Eastern Airlines flight departed from Miami, bound for the Bahamas. Shortly after takeoff, one of the plane's three jet engines lost oil pressure. The flight crew shut down the failing engine and turned the plane around. Soon thereafter, the second and third engines failed due to loss of oil pressure. The plane began losing altitude rapidly, and the passengers were told that the plane would be ditched in the Atlantic Ocean. Fortunately, the pilot somehow managed to restart an engine and land the plane safely at the airport.

A number of the (apparently ungrateful) passengers brought actions against the airline, claiming damages for mental distress arising out of the incident. The district court entertained each complaint in a consolidated proceeding. Eastern conceded that the engine failure and the subsequent preparations for a crash landing constituted an "accident" under Article 17 of the Warsaw Convention, but argued that physical injury was a condition of liability.

Relying on another federal court's analysis of the French text and negotiating history of the Convention, the district court concluded that mental anguish alone was not compensable. The Eleventh Circuit reversed the holding of the district court, holding that the phrase *lesion corporelle*, "bodily injury," *did* encompass purely emotional distress. To supports its conclusion, the court examined the French legal meaning of the term, the concurrent and subsequent history of the Convention, and cases interpreting the article.

The Supreme Court granted certiorari to resolve a conflict between the Eleventh Circuit's decision in this case and that of the New York Court of Appeals, which held that purely psychic trauma was not compensable under Article 17.

TREATY INTERPRETATION

As it turns out, the only authentic text of the Warsaw Convention was written in French, which guided the Court's analysis. The American translation, employed by the Senate when it ratified the Convention in 1934, reads as follows:

> The carrier shall be liable for damage sustained *in the event of the death or wounding of a passenger or any other bodily injury* suffered by a passenger, if the accident which caused the damage so sustained took place on board the aircraft or in the course of any of the operations of embarking or disembarking [emphasis added].

Thus, an air carrier is liable for passenger injury only when three conditions are satisfied: (1) there has been an accident, in which (2) the passenger suffered *mort*, "death," *blessure*, "wound," or *lesion corporelle*, "bodily injury," and (3) the accident took place on board the aircraft or in the course of operations of embarking or disembarking.

The airline conceded that the incident took place on board the aircraft and was an "accident." The plaintiffs conceded that they suffered neither *mort* nor *blessure* from the mishap. Therefore, the narrow issue presented to the court was whether *lesion corporelle* was satisfied when a passenger has suffered only a mental injury.

The court closely examined the French legal meaning of *lesion corporelle*, because the Convention was drafted in French by continental jurists. The simplest method of determining the meaning of a foreign phrase is to consult a bilingual dictionary. These dictionaries clearly define *lesion corporelle* as "bodily injury." The translation used by the U.S. Senate when ratifying the Warsaw Convention also equated *lesion corporelle* with "bodily injury." And the same wording appeared in the translation used in the United Kingdom Carriage by Air Act of 1932.

The Supreme Court then turned to French legal materials to determine whether French jurists' contemporary understanding of the term *lesion corporelle* somehow differed from its translated meaning. In 1929, lawyers trained in French civil law would have relied on legislation, judicial decisions, and scholarly writing. The Court's review of these materials indicated that *lesion corporelle* was not a widely used legal term in French law, and that the term did not specifically encompass psychic injuries. The Court did not find any French legislative provisions in 1929 that contained the phrase *lesion corporelle*, and the Court likewise discovered no French court decisions that explained the phrase *lesion corporelle*. Indeed, the Court found no French case construing this article of the Warsaw Convention to cover psychic injury.

The Court then turned to French treatises and scholarly writing prior to the Warsaw Convention, and it found no materials indicating that *lesion corporelle* included psychic injury. The Court remarked that scholars who advocated that the term encompassed psychic injury did not base their argument on French cases, codes, or treatises, but on the principle of French tort law that any damage can give rise to reparation "when it is real and has been verified."

In sum, neither the Warsaw Convention itself nor any of the applicable French legal sources revealed that *lesion corporelle* should be translated other than as "bodily injury." However, because a broader interpretation was theoretically plausible, the Court examined additional aids to construction.

CONSTRUCTION AIDS

The Supreme Court's review of the documentary record for the Warsaw Conference confirmed that there was no evidence that the drafters or signatories of the Warsaw Convention specifically considered liability for psychic injury or the meaning of *lesion corporelle*. Two explanations commonly were offered for why the subject of mental injuries never arose during those proceedings: (1) many jurisdictions did not recognize recovery for mental injury at that time, and (2) the drafters simply could not contemplate a psychic injury unaccompanied by a physical injury.

The unavailability of compensation for purely psychic injury in many common and civil law countries at the time of the Warsaw Conference persuaded the Court that the signatories had no intention of including such a remedy.

Because such a remedy was unknown in many, if not most, jurisdictions in 1929, the drafters most likely would have made a clear reference to purely mental injury if they had intended to allow such recovery.

The Court also reasoned that a narrower reading of *lesion corporelle* was consistent with the primary purpose of the contracting parties to the Convention: limiting the liability of air carriers in order to foster the growth of the fledgling commercial aviation industry. Indeed, it was for this reason that the Warsaw delegates imposed a maximum recovery of $8,300 for an accident, which was a fairly meager amount even by 1929 standards. The delegates were more concerned with protecting air carriers and fostering a new industry than with providing full recovery to injured passengers. The Court therefore concluded that an air carrier could not be held liable when an accident has not caused a passenger to suffer death, physical injury, or physical manifestation of injury. The Court expressed no view as to whether passengers could recover for mental injuries when accompanied by physical injuries.

The judgment of the court of appeals was accordingly reversed, reminding passengers on aircraft with failing engines to (a) keep a stiff upper lip, and (b) forget about compensation if the plane doesn't crash.

7

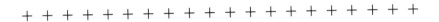

CASH STASH
THE LIMITS OF LIABILITY

*REPUBLIC NATIONAL BANK OF
NEW YORK V. EASTERN AIRLINES*
815 F.2d 232 (2nd Cir. 1987)

Much to its chagrin, Republic National Bank discovered that currency really doesn't weigh all that much, thereby severely limiting an airline's liability when it misplaces a huge wad of cash. In this case, Republic lost $2 million in checked luggage, and in return it received $634.90 in settlement from Eastern Airlines. The bank—it is safe to say—was not amused.

Republic brought this action to recover the currency lost on an Eastern flight from New York to Lima, Peru. In response, Eastern filed a motion for summary judgment alleging that its liability was limited by the Warsaw Convention to $9.07 per pound. Republic opposed summary judgment on the grounds (a) that Eastern failed to comply with the baggage claim check requirements of the Convention, and (b) that the airline was guilty of willful misconduct in handling Republic's baggage, thereby vitiating its claim to limited liability.

After hearing arguments, the district judge granted Eastern's motion for summary judgment, holding that the airline's liability was in fact limited by the Convention. Republic, of course, appealed.

COURSE OF CURRENCY

As part of its service to South American customers, Republic operated an in-house courier service for the transportation of currency as checked baggage. In May of 1982, representatives of Republic met with Eastern officials to discuss Eastern's flight schedule for its newly acquired South American routes. At this meeting, Republic informed Eastern that couriers would be accompanying large amounts of currency shipped as checked baggage. Eastern responded that it would not accept liability for high-value cargo shipped as checked baggage. But Eastern did agree to provide Republic with a customer assistance letter to facilitate Republic's use of the airline's services.

On December 13, 1982, Republic instructed Renzo Baronti, an international courier, to accompany two bags of currency aboard Eastern Flight 001. One bag, bound for Lima, contained $2 million. The second bag, containing $4.5 million, was to be delivered to Santiago, Chile. Flight 001 was to stop in Miami, Florida, en route to its first South American stop in Lima.

Baronti obtained a ticket from an Eastern ticket agent at John F. Kennedy Airport, which bore a notice of the Warsaw Convention's applicability. Baronti then proceeded to the Eastern baggage check area and informed an attendant that he was accompanying a "high value shipment" and required two baggage claim checks. Baronti did not otherwise make a special declaration as to the value of his shipment, nor did he reveal its contents. The Eastern attendant made no effort to verify the presence of Baronti's bags, which were being driven to the aircraft in a Wells Fargo armored truck.

Baronti received two claim checks from the attendant. The claim check for the Santiago bag was a standard claim check containing the destination, baggage identification number, preprinted routing codes, and notice of the Warsaw Convention's applicability. Because the attendant could not find a standard Lima claim check, a limited release form was substituted, but it did not contain the routing codes or Warsaw Convention notice. The attendant wrote Baronti's name on the limited release and handed him both claim checks. Baronti then added "FLT # 1 LIMA" to the limited release and proceeded to the boarding area.

Baronti informed Eastern's gate agents that he was a courier accompanying a high-value shipment and requested access to the tarmac to meet the armored car. Eastern complied with this request. At planeside, the Wells Fargo armored truck arrived under escort by Eastern. Baronti entered the truck, checked the seals and locks on the bags, and affixed the Santiago claim check to the bag containing $4.5 million. He affixed the limited release form to the Lima bag containing $2 million.

Both bags were then loaded aboard the plane. Although Baronti instructed Eastern employees to load Republic's bags last, several carts of late cargo were loaded after Republic's shipment was secured. Baronti did not register any objection to this procedure. Upon the flight's arrival in Miami, Eastern allowed Baronti to leave the aircraft first. Baronti met armed guards at planeside and observed Eastern personnel unloading cargo and baggage. Both bags were visually inspected to Baronti's satisfaction and were replaced in the cargo bin. Eastern flight 001 then proceeded to Lima, where Baronti discovered to his astonishment that the bag containing $2 million was missing. Six weeks later, five suspects were arrested in Atlantic City with approximately $150,000 of the missing currency in their possession.

LIABILITY LIMITATIONS

The Warsaw Convention is a comprehensive international treaty whose purpose is to create uniform rules limiting airline liability for damages resulting from personal injury or property damage. As a quid pro quo for limiting recovery, the treaty creates a presumption of airline liability in favor of passengers. Thus, a passenger may hold an airline strictly liable for damages suffered in international transportation, but recovery of damages is limited by various provisions of the Convention. (The provisions of the Warsaw Convention have now been largely superseded by those of the Montreal Convention.)

With respect to checked baggage, Article 18 provides for the strict liability of carriers for loss or damage. Article 22(2) limits the carrier's liability to $20 per kilogram or $9.07 per pound. The limitation of damages only applies if the carrier has delivered a baggage claim check in conformity with the extensive requirements of Article 4 of the Warsaw Convention, which requires a carrier to provide a passenger with a baggage claim check containing certain information:

1. For the transportation of baggage, other than small personal objects of which the passenger takes charge himself, the carrier must deliver a baggage check.

2. The baggage check shall be made out in duplicate, one part for the passenger and the other part for the carrier.

3. The baggage check shall contain the following particulars:
   a. The place and date of issue;
   b. The place of departure and of destination;
   c. The name and address of the carrier or carriers;
   d. The number of the passenger ticket;
   e. A statement that delivery of the baggage will be made to the bearer of the baggage check;
   f. The number and weight of the packages;
   g. The amount of the value declared in accordance with article 2(2);
   h. A statement that the transportation is subject to the rules relating to liability established by this convention.

4. The absence, irregularity, or loss of the baggage check shall not affect the existence or the validity of the contract of transportation which shall nonetheless be subject to the rules of this convention. Nevertheless, if the carrier accepts baggage without a baggage check having been delivered, or if the baggage check does not contain the particulars set out at (*d*), (*f*), and (*h*) above, the carrier shall not be entitled to avail himself of those provisions of the convention which exclude or limit his liability.

Under the express terms of Article 4, limited liability is precluded in the absence of either the passenger ticket number, the number and weight of the packages, or the required notice. All three of these items were missing from the limited release form handed to Republic's courier. But in the appellate court's view, the absence of the printed notice and weight of the bag did not prejudice Republic for the following reasons.

First, with respect to notice of the Convention's applicability, the district court found that Baronti was an experienced courier, having made over 250 flights. Republic could not therefore reasonably contend that Baronti was unaware of the Warsaw Convention. Additionally, a proper notice was printed both on Baronti's passenger ticket and on his baggage claim check for the Santiago bag.

Second, the failure of Eastern to record the weight of Republic's baggage on the limited release was not prejudicial. The purpose of the weight requirement is to enable passengers to calculate the amount recoverable from the carrier under the Warsaw Convention for lost or damaged baggage. A passenger need only multiply the amount recoverable per pound under the Convention ($9.07) by the weight of his baggage to arrive at this figure. Once having made the calculation, a passenger has enough information to decide whether to purchase insurance.

In the case at bar, Republic must have known that it could not obtain recovery for $2 million under the Convention, even if Baronti did not know the precise weight of his bag. In order to recover $2 million at $9.07 per pound, Republic's currency bag would have to weigh 220,507 pounds! Obviously, Republic was on notice that insurance coverage would be necessary to adequately protect its shipment.

The absence of a baggage identification number on the release, the court said, was more troubling. The obvious purpose of the baggage identification number is to ensure recovery of a passenger's baggage. But several factors indicated that Republic was not prejudiced by the absence of an identification number. First, the Republic courier did not present his baggage to Eastern's attendant at the baggage check counter. Instead, Republic's currency bags were located in an armored truck parked on the tarmac. As a result, Eastern had no opportunity to ensure that Republic's baggage was properly identified. Second, Republic's courier personally supervised the handling of the currency bags at each point in the journey. This supervision virtually eliminated the possibility that Eastern mishandled the bank's bag as a result of the missing identification number. Eastern personnel easily located Republic's currency bag in Miami. After carefully viewing the bag, Baronti identified it as belonging to Republic. For these reasons, Republic could not claim that the absence of an identification number was prejudicial.

WILLFUL MISCONDUCT

As an alternative theory, Republic argued that Eastern should not be allowed to claim limited liability because Eastern was guilty of willful misconduct in handling its baggage. Republic relied on Article 25(1) of the Warsaw Convention, which provides:

> The carrier shall not be entitled to avail himself of the provisions of this convention which exclude or limit his liability, if the damage is caused by his willful misconduct or by such default on his part as, in accordance with the law of the court to which the case is submitted, is considered to be equivalent to willful misconduct.

Willful misconduct requires either (a) the intentional performance of an act with knowledge that the performance of that act will probably result in injury, or (b) the intentional performance of an act in such a manner as to imply reckless disregard of the probable consequences. If Republic was to benefit from Article 25(1), it had to satisfy its burden by proving that Eastern had acted in reckless disregard of the probable consequences of its acts in loading Republic's baggage in New York.

Republic claimed that Eastern committed willful misconduct in three ways: (1) Eastern violated its own tariff by accepting currency as checked baggage, (2) Eastern failed to adopt formal security procedures for the loading of high-value baggage, and (3) Eastern violated its own de facto procedures when handling the bank's baggage. The appellate court agreed with the district court that no genuine issue of material fact existed.

THE BANK'S CLAIMS

Rule 16A(2) of Eastern's tariff provided that "fragile or perishable articles, *money,* jewelry, silverware, negotiable papers, securities or other valuables will not be accepted as checked baggage" [emphasis added]. Republic contended that Eastern was guilty of willful misconduct because it failed to "take appropriate measures for the bag's protection" after accepting Republic's currency in violation of its tariff. The appellate court did not agree.

Even if Eastern knowingly accepted currency as checked baggage, the court was not prepared to hold that an airline's mere violation of its tariff, without more, was sufficient to permit a finding of willful misconduct. Willful misconduct requires performance of an act in reckless disregard of the probable consequences.

The simple acceptance of currency as checked baggage did not alone create a probability of its loss. Other factors had to be established indicating that such a loss was likely to occur and that the airline was aware of the probability when it accepted the plaintiff's valuables. According to the court, Republic failed to produce any evidence that the mere acceptance of its currency as checked baggage was likely to result in loss and that Eastern was aware of this likelihood.

Republic argued that Eastern committed willful misconduct by failing to adopt formal procedures for handling "high value baggage." Eastern had formal security procedures only for items designated "high value cargo," but Eastern provided this service for an extra charge. Republic chose not to pay the additional fee and could not later complain that the choice was unwise.

Republic finally contended that Eastern was guilty of willful misconduct for failure to follow certain customary procedures in loading Republic's baggage from armored cars. According to Republic, Eastern would customarily load Republic's bags last to ensure that they would be the first items unloaded. On the occasion of the loss, Eastern loaded additional baggage after loading Republic's currency bags. Republic claimed that the placement of Republic's bag in the interior of the hold facilitated its disappearance.

Although Republic alleged that Eastern developed the last-on, first-off procedure, the testimony of Republic's own courier revealed that it was Republic who suggested the practice. When Flight 001 arrived in Miami, Eastern personnel displayed both Republic bags for visual inspection by the courier. At that time, the courier was satisfied that the currency bags were safely aboard the aircraft. At no time did he object to the location of the currency bags in the cargo bin, nor did he request that the bags be moved closer to the door. Because Republic failed to produce any evidence from which a reasonable jury could find that willful misconduct caused Republic's loss, the appellate court affirmed the summary judgment in favor of Eastern.

In the end, the bank could only console itself with the fact that it could deduct from its $2 million loss the measly sum of $634.09 that it received from the airline for lost luggage.

8

+ + + + + + + + + + + + + + + + + + +

BOARDING DENIED

A QUESTION OF SECURITY

+ + + + + + + + + + + + + + + + + + +

SMITH V. COMAIR
134 F.3d 254 (4th Cir. 1998)

On the morning of October 5, 1995—long before the tragic events of September 11, 2001, and its resulting terrorist security precautions—James Smith boarded a 6:40 a.m. Comair flight in Roanoke, Virginia, to travel to Minneapolis, with a brief layover in Cincinnati. Comair representatives did not ask Smith for proof of identification when he boarded the flight in Roanoke.

In Cincinnati, Smith met some business associates, and together they were to take the 9:00 a.m. connecting flight to Minneapolis. When Smith began to board the plane, the Comair representative asked him to step aside. After watching the rest of the passengers board, Smith asked why he was detained.

A Comair representative told Smith that a supervisor would be summoned. The supervisor, a Mr. Price, arrived approximately 30 minutes after the Minneapolis flight departed. Price would not explain why Smith could not board the flight. Meanwhile, Smith noticed that two security guards standing nearby were watching him closely.

Several hours later, Price finally told Smith that he was denied permission to board the Minneapolis flight because he did not match the physical description in his Delta frequent-flyer account. Smith called his travel agent and discovered that the airline did not maintain such a record. Smith confronted Price with this information, and Price continued to insist that the dissimilar physical description was the reason he was not allowed to board.

At 2:00 p.m., Price returned to Smith and told him the real reason he was refused permission to board was that the Roanoke agent had failed to ask for photo identification, as shown by the absence of pink highlighting on his boarding pass. Price explained that the FAA required photo identification for security reasons, and Smith replied that he could not produce his driver's license because he had left it in the glove compartment of his car, which was parked at the Roanoke airport. Smith offered to have his physical description faxed by the Virginia Department of Motor Vehicles or to pay Comair's expenses if they would open his car, retrieve his driver's license, and deliver it to Cincinnati on the available flight. Price refused both options, as the DMV could not fax a photo and entering Smith's car would expose Comair to liability.

Finally, at about 3:00 p.m., Price agreed to return Smith to Roanoke. While waiting to board the flight, Smith told Price he was so angry he would like to "punch him in the mouth." In response, Price motioned to the security guards. When the two approached, Price asked them to remove Smith from the terminal. After Smith explained his situation, one officer intervened and convinced Price to let Smith to fly to Roanoke, which he did.

In due course, Smith sued the airline, alleging breach of contract, false imprisonment, and intentional infliction of emotional distress. Comair argued that Smith's claims were preempted by the Airline Deregulation Act (ADA) and, alternatively, that his intentional tort claims should be dismissed for failure to state a claim. The district court agreed that Smith's contract and tort claims were preempted as regards Comair's boarding procedures. Furthermore, to the extent Smith's tort claims rested on other allegations, the court agreed that they should also be dismissed.

SAFETY CONCERNS

The scope of federal preemption under the ADA was new to the Fourth Circuit. The court noted that when Congress passed the act, it granted broad discretion to airlines in making safety-related boarding decisions. The statute provided in part: "Subject to regulations of the Administrator, an air carrier, intrastate air carrier, or foreign air carrier may refuse to transport a passenger or property the carrier decides is, or might be, inimical to safety."

The court explained that air travel presents formidable safety and security concerns and passengers with criminal intentions are often the source of that threat. Federal law—in conjunction with its broad preemption of state-law claims related to airlines' services—appropriately allowed the airlines wide latitude in making decisions necessary to safeguard passengers from potential security threats.

BREACH OF CONTRACT

Smith contended that by refusing him permission to board his flight, Comair breached a general contractual duty to transport him to Minneapolis. The appellate court held that Smith failed to appreciate the effect that Comair's federal defenses had on the preemption question. Because the airline invoked defenses provided by federal law, Smith's contract claim could only be adjudicated by reference to law and to policies external to the parties' bargain, and therefore it too was preempted under the ADA.

The court explained that state contract claims escape preemption only when courts would be confined to the terms of the parties' agreement. Here Comair invoked federal law in two respects. First, the airline argued that it was entitled to prevent Smith from boarding by the federal statute granting just such discretion for safety-related reasons. Second, Comair asserted that it had a legal duty to refuse Smith permission to board under heightened FAA security directives that became effective the evening before Smith's flight. In response to those directives, the airline required that ticketed passengers between the ages of 18 and 60 present either official photo identification issued by a government authority or two forms of identification, one of which had to be issued by a government agency.

Smith's failure to produce identification implicated the safety concerns of both the ADA and the FAA directive. Because Smith's contract claim was based upon Comair's refusal to permit him to board, it directly implicated the airline's discretion and/or duty under federal law. Accordingly, the contract claim was preempted under the ADA. Allowing Smith's claim to proceed would frustrate this important federal objective because airlines might hesitate to heed potentially dangerous signals for fear of lawsuits alleging refusal to transport.

INTENTIONAL TORTS

Smith next contended that his false imprisonment and intentional infliction of emotional distress claims were not preempted. He admitted that an airline's boarding practices were properly considered a "service," which preempted state laws, but he argued that tort claims were not preempted if premised upon unreasonable conduct that was unnecessary to the provision of a service. He characterized Comair's conduct during his encounter as so outrageous as to be unrelated to the provision of a service.

To the extent Smith's intentional tort claims were premised on Comair's refusal to permit him to board his flight, the appellate court concluded that they were preempted. But the appellate court agreed with Smith that, to the extent his claims were based on conduct distinct from Comair's determination not to grant permission to board, his false imprisonment and intentional infliction of emotional distress claims were not preempted. Suits stemming from outrageous conduct on the part of an airline toward a passenger are not preempted under the ADA if the conduct was too tenuously related to an airline's services, the court said.

As for the false imprisonment claim, Smith's evidence simply did not reveal that he was compelled to remain. He conceded that the Comair representative never told him that he must remain in a specific part of the airport or that he was not free to leave the airport. Price told Smith only that Comair would not permit him to board the flight out of Cincinnati. Smith was therefore free to leave the airport or to leave Cincinnati altogether by any other means he could arrange. False imprisonment, the court said, results only if the restraint is a total one, rather than a mere obstruction of the right to go where the plaintiff pleases.

Smith next contended that Price's outrageous behavior—lying and rudely failing to assist Smith—constituted intentional infliction of emotional distress. The appellate court disagreed. The Kentucky Supreme Court had previously held that the conduct must be outrageous and intolerable in that it offends "generally accepted standards of decency and morality." In the court's view, Price's conduct was unquestionably rude and unprofessional, but was not so outrageous as to satisfy this high standard. Comair had doubtless lost the goodwill of a customer, but it did not commit a tort. Even Smith conceded that the incident had almost no effect on his life: "Personally it has not affected me." Because Smith failed to satisfy at least two elements of an intentional infliction of emotional distress action, the appellate court found that the district court properly granted summary judgment in favor of Comair.

And Mr. Smith will undoubtedly remember to bring his identification the next time he flew out of Cincinnati.

9

+ + + + + + + + + + + + + + + + + +

GUNS ON BOARD

AN ISSUE OF AIRLINE SAFETY

+ + + + + + + + + + + + + + + + + +

AIR WISCONSIN V. HOEPER
134 S.Ct. 852 (2014)

William Hoeper was hired as a pilot for Air Wisconsin in 1998. By late 2004, the airline had stopped operating flights from Denver, Hoeper's home base, with the type of aircraft for which he was certified. To continue flying for the airline, Hoeper needed to obtain certification on the British Aerospace 146, a plane that he had not previously flown.

Hoeper failed his first three attempts to pass a proficiency test for the new aircraft. His employment was now at the discretion of Air Wisconsin, but the airline agreed to give him one more chance. The agreement left little doubt that Hoeper would lose his job if he failed the test.

In December 2004, Hoeper flew from Denver to Virginia for simulator training as part of this final exam. During the training, Hoeper mishandled a challenging situation, and the simulator showed that the engines exploded due to loss of fuel. As the instructor was about to tell Hoeper he should have known better, Hoeper went into a rage, as he later testified:

At this point, that's it. I take my headset off and I toss it up on the glare shield. The instructor and I exchanged words at the same elevated decibel level. Mine went something like this: "This is a bunch of s**t. I'm sorry. You are railroading the situation and it's not realistic."

When Hoeper announced he wanted to call the legal department of the pilots' union, the session was terminated. The instructor then reported Hoeper's behavior to a manager, who booked him on a United Airlines flight back to Denver.

Shortly thereafter, the situation was discussed by several executives at Air Wisconsin, who were concerned what Hoeper might do next, especially in light of the fact that he was about to be terminated. It was also worrisome that Hoeper was a federal flight deck officer, which allowed him to carry a firearm on board an aircraft in order to defend against acts of criminal violence or piracy. Furthermore, the Denver airport's security procedures allowed for crew members to bypass screening. As a result, one of the airline's executives called the Transportation Safety Administration (TSA) to inform them of the situation.

The TSA responded to the call by ordering Hoeper's plane to return to the gate. Officers boarded the plane, removed Hoeper, searched him, and questioned him about his gun. When he replied that the gun was at his home, a local federal agent went there to retrieve it. Hoeper took a later flight to Denver, and the next day, the airline fired him.

THE LAWSUIT

Hoeper sued Air Wisconsin in Colorado state court on several claims, including defamation. Air Wisconsin moved for summary judgment on the basis of immunity under the Aviation and Transportation Security Act (ATSA), but the trial court denied the motion, ruling that the jury was entitled to hear the facts. The case went to trial, and the judge submitted the issue of ATSA immunity to the jury, with the instruction that immunity would not apply if Air Wisconsin had made the disclosure to the TSA with knowledge that it was "false, inaccurate, or misleading" or "with reckless disregard as to its truth or falsity."

The jury found for Hoeper on the defamation claim and awarded him $849,625 in compensatory damages and $391,875 in punitive damages (which the court reduced to $350,000), for a total judgment of about $1.2 million, plus costs. The Colorado Court of Appeals affirmed, holding that the trial court properly submitted the ATSA immunity issue to the jury, that the record supported the jury's rejection of immunity, and that the evidence was sufficient to support the jury's defamation verdict.

The Colorado Supreme Court affirmed. It held that immunity under the ATSA was a question of law to be determined by the trial court before trial, but it concluded that the trial court's error in submitting immunity to the jury was harmless because the airline was not entitled to immunity. The court stated: "In our determination of immunity under the ATSA, we need not, and therefore do not, decide whether the statements were true or false. Rather, we conclude that Air Wisconsin made the statements with reckless disregard as to their truth or falsity."

The court noted that Air Wisconsin would likely be immune under the ATSA if the airline's manager had simply reported that Hoeper was an Air Wisconsin employee, that he knew he would be terminated soon, that he had acted irrationally at the training three hours earlier by "blowing up" at a test administrator, and that he was a federal flight deck officer who was allowed to carry a gun. But because the airline manager actually told the TSA: (1) that he believed Hoeper to be mentally unstable, (2) that Hoeper had been terminated earlier that day, and (3) that Hoeper may have been armed, the court determined that his statements went beyond the facts and therefore did not qualify for immunity. The court concluded that the evidence was sufficient to support the jury's defamation verdict.

The U.S. Supreme Court granted certiorari to decide whether ATSA immunity could be denied without a determination that the air carrier's disclosure was materially false.

TSA IMMUNITY

In 2001, Congress created the TSA to assess and manage threats against air travel. To ensure that the TSA would be informed of potential threats, Congress gave airlines and their employees immunity against civil liability for reporting suspicious behavior. But this immunity did not attach to any disclosure made with "actual knowledge that the disclosure was false, inaccurate, or misleading" or any disclosure made with "reckless disregard as to the truth or falsity of that disclosure."

The question before the U.S. Supreme Court was whether ATSA immunity may be denied without a determination that a disclosure was materially false, and the Court concluded that it may not. Because the state courts in this case made no such determination, and because any falsehood in the disclosure at issue would not have affected a reasonable security officer's assessment of the supposed threat, the Court reversed the judgment of the Colorado Supreme Court.

It soon became apparent to the Court that Congress had patterned the exception to ATSA immunity after the actual malice standard set forth in the landmark defamation case of *New York Times Co. v. Sullivan,* which held that under the First Amendment, a public figure cannot recover for a defamatory falsehood relating to his conduct unless he proves that the statement was made with "actual malice," that is, with knowledge that it was false or with reckless disregard of whether it was false or not. Congress used this exact language in denying ATSA immunity to (1) any disclosure made with actual knowledge that the disclosure was false, inaccurate, or misleading or (2) any disclosure made with reckless disregard as to the truth or falsity of that disclosure. Thus, a statement otherwise eligible for ATSA immunity may not be denied immunity unless the statement is materially false.

Such a requirement also serves the purpose of ATSA immunity, the Court explained. The ATSA shifted from airlines to the TSA the responsibility for assessing and investigating possible threats to airline security. In directing the TSA to receive, assess, and distribute intelligence information related to transportation security, Congress wanted to ensure that air carriers and their employees would not hesitate to provide the TSA with the information it needed. This is the purpose of the immunity provision, and denying immunity for substantially true reports on the theory that the person making the report had not yet gathered enough information to be certain of its truth would defeat the purpose. Such a rule would restore the previous state of affairs in which air carriers bore the responsibility to investigate and verify potential threats.

The U.S. Supreme Court held that by incorporating the actual malice standard into the statute, Congress meant to give air carriers the "breathing space" to report potential threats to security officials without fear of civil liability for "a few inaptly chosen words." To hold Air Wisconsin liable for minor misstatements or loose wording would undermine the very purpose of the act and disregard the statutory text.

The judgment of the Colorado Supreme Court in favor of the plaintiff was therefore reversed and the case remanded for further proceedings.

10

+ + + + + + + + + + + + + + + + + +

A LITTLE OUT
OF HAND

MINDING THE GATE AGENT

+ + + + + + + + + + + + + + + + + +

CHRISSAFIS V. CONTINENTAL AIRLINES
940 F. Supp. 1292 (N.D. Ill. 1996)

Catherine Chrissafis purchased a round-trip airline ticket from Continental Airlines to transport her from Newark to Chicago and then back to Newark. After spending time in Chicago, Chrissafis was driven by a friend to O'Hare International Airport, where she boarded Continental Flight 1275 for her return trip. After taking her seat, Chrissafis realized she still had her friend's car keys.

Chrissafis could see through the airplane window that her friend was still in the boarding area (this was obviously back in the days when security was less stringent). In an attempt to return the keys, Chrissafis asked a flight attendant for permission to deplane. The flight attendant told Chrissafis that she could return the keys if she did so quickly, because the flight was about to depart. As Chrissafis walked up the ramp to the terminal, another Continental employee stopped her and asked where she was going. Chrissafis explained the situation, and the employee told Chrissafis that she could return the keys and reboard the aircraft.

Chrissafis continued up the ramp back to the boarding area where her friend was waiting. As Chrissafis stepped through the door, she waved to her friend and told him to come pick up his keys. As her friend approached, a Continental employee named Burgess approached Chrissafis and demanded to know what she was doing. She explained that two Continental employees had given her permission to return the keys to her friend and reboard the aircraft. Burgess closed the door to the plane and, despite Chrissafis's protestations, refused to allow her to reboard the flight.

As Burgess leaned forward to lock the door to the aircraft, her forearm collided with Chrissafis's forearm. At that point, Burgess declared that she was going to call the police and have Chrissafis arrested. As Burgess called the police, one of the Continental employees who had allowed Chrissafis to exit the aircraft opened the gateway door from the other side. That employee instructed Chrissafis to follow her back onto the aircraft, which she did.

Burgess objected and followed Chrissafis and the crew member down the ramp to the airplane. Once aboard the airplane, both Chrissafis and Burgess told their stories to the pilot. The pilot instructed Chrissafis to retrieve her carry-on belongings and exit the plane. By the time Chrissafis returned to the boarding area, four Chicago police officers had arrived. Burgess told the police officers her version of what happened, and Chrissafis was arrested for battery. She was placed in a holding cell at O'Hare and then transported to a Chicago police precinct, where officers photographed and fingerprinted her. She was then strip-searched and incarcerated in a cell at the police station. She remained incarcerated for several hours until bail could be posted.

A hearing was held on the criminal complaint filed by Burgess. Chrissafis retained counsel, returned to Chicago, and appeared at the hearing. Burgess did not appear at the hearing, and the court dismissed the battery charge.

Chrissafis then sued Continental for false arrest, false imprisonment, and intentional infliction of emotional distress. Continental moved to dismiss the complaint on the grounds that state tort and contract claims were preempted by the Airline Deregulation Act (ADA).

FALSE ARREST AND FALSE IMPRISONMENT

Several courts have addressed the issue of whether the ADA preempts false arrest and false imprisonment claims, and the results were clearly divergent. Those cases concluding that the ADA preempts false arrest and false imprisonment claims involved incidents in which the airline refused or failed to provide a service to a passenger. In one case, a passenger confined to a wheelchair brought a false imprisonment claim after he was denied admittance to a flight and then strapped to an immobile chair in the airline waiting area. The court held that because the plaintiff's objective was to fly on the defendant's airplane, the claim related to services and was preempted. In another case, the plaintiff was detained by airline personnel and was forced to purchase a new ticket because the airline believed the passenger was traveling with a stolen ticket. The court held that the plaintiff's false arrest and false imprisonment claims were preempted because they were "clearly related to airline services." In these cases, where the crux of the claim was the airline's refusal to transport the passenger, the courts concluded that the claims related to the provision of services and were therefore preempted by the ADA.

In contrast, where the gist of the false arrest and false imprisonment claim was that the airline caused the passenger to be arrested by authorities without a proper factual basis, courts have held that the claims are *not* related to services and are therefore not preempted. In one case, the court permitted a passenger to pursue a claim that airline personnel falsely identified the passenger as an illegal alien, causing police and customs agents to arrest and detain her. In another case, the court allowed a claim that the flight crew had falsely arrested the passenger for smoking marijuana, causing him to be strip-searched, threatened, and detained for several hours. In yet another case, the court refused to preempt a passenger's claim that an airline pilot made misrepresentations to police, causing the plaintiff to be taken into custody, detained, and subjected to a luggage search. These courts concluded that an airline's false arrest and imprisonment of a passenger did not constitute a "service" within the preemptive scope of the ADA. As one court quipped, tortious conduct of an airline is not a typical "service" provided by the airline industry.

In the court's view, Chrissafis's allegations were similar to the facts in the second line of cases. Chrissafis claimed that Burgess's statements to the Chicago police were false and caused her to be arrested and imprisoned without grounds to believe that she had committed a criminal offense. Her false arrest and imprisonment claims did not focus on Continental's refusal or failure to provide a service. Instead, she centered her false arrest and false imprisonment claims around Burgess's bogus statements to law enforcement officials. These actions simply did not relate to airline services.

The court reasoned that furnishing false information to police and thereby causing a false arrest and incarceration are not part of a contractual arrangement between an airline and its passenger. Nor does causing a false arrest reasonably further the provision of an airline service. Because these actions exceeded the scope of the agreement between an airline and passenger, they did not constitute services within the meaning of the ADA.

The court noted that its holding was consistent with the ADA's purpose of preempting state economic regulation of the airline industry. The ADA was intended to preempt economic regulation of airlines by states and was not a safe harbor for airlines from civil tort claims. Allowing her tort claim to proceed would not significantly affect Continental's rates, routes, or services. Any economic effect this suit may have on Continental was "too tenuous, remote, or peripheral" to justify preemption. Additionally, this holding was consistent with Congress's decision to retain the Savings Clause to protect the states' ability to control noneconomic matters concerning airlines within their state.

INTENTIONAL INFLICTION OF EMOTIONAL DISTRESS

The plaintiff's complaint did not make clear whether Chrissafis's emotional distress was the result of the airline's refusal to allow her to board or the consequence of her arrest and imprisonment. Chrissafis's claim would be preempted, the court said, were it based only on the allegation that Continental forced her to exit the aircraft and refused to transport her to Newark. Nevertheless, the courts allowed Chrissafis to proceed with her emotional distress claim to the extent that it was based on the allegation that the airline provided false information leading to her arrest and imprisonment. Accordingly, the airline's motion to dismiss the emotional distress claim was denied.

The court ordered the parties to discuss settlement before the next court date, and the case somehow quietly disappeared.

11

+ + + + + + + + + + + + + + + + + + + +

DEPLANED!
PUSHING THE BOUNDARIES
OF PILOT DISCRETION

+ + + + + + + + + + + + + + + + + + + +

EID V. ALASKA AIRLINES
621 F.3d 858 (9th Cir. 2010)

In September of 2003, a group of Egyptian businessmen, their wives, and a fiancée boarded Alaska Airlines Flight 694 in Vancouver, British Columbia. Their journey had begun a few days earlier in Cairo, and they were headed to Las Vegas to attend a convention.

The nine plaintiffs took up all but three of the first-class seats on the flight. A tenth passenger was Kimberlie Shealy, an American, who sat next to one of the plaintiffs, whom she described as "a gentleman." According to Shealy, who provided the only independent account of the incident being litigated, the flight attendants treated the Egyptians very poorly.

About an hour into the flight, passenger Reda Ginena, who was in the front row with his wife and son, stood up to stretch. One of the flight attendants asked him to take his seat because standing was prohibited outside the cockpit. Ginena, who was in his 60s, explained that he needed to stretch periodically, because certain medical problems made protracted sitting painful. The flight attendant said he could do so at the rear of the first-class cabin.

Ginena moved there, but another flight attendant told him to sit down in what Shealy described as "an unpleasant loud voice." According to Shealy, the flight attendant "glared" at the Egyptians but no one else. Ginena claimed that "the flight attendant went ballistic and began pacing between the first row and the galley and yelling. She was completely irrational."

Shealy testified that she saw no misconduct by the passengers or any indication they were intoxicated. According to her, they "were being accused of something that they clearly did not understand and were being humiliated before the entire aircraft as the flight attendant was yelling at the top of her lungs." Ginena finally told the flight attendant that she couldn't treat him that way, to which the flight attendant responded, "I will show you what I can do. I'm taking this plane down." All conversation stopped, and the flight attendant picked up the phone to call the captain.

Captain Michel Swanigan testified that the flight attendant said, "I've got some passengers giving me a bit of a problem here in first class. I'd like to have security meet the airplane when we get in." The captain responded, "Is there anything urgent, anything we need to know?" The flight attendant replied, "No, I think I've got it under control." Following the conversation, the captain put the aircraft into "lockdown mode" and turned on the "fasten seat belt" sign.

Minutes later, Captain Swanigan received a second call from the flight attendant. According to the captain: "She came across distraught; almost sounded like she was crying, and said, 'Mike, I've lost control of the first-class cabin.' And when I heard that, also I heard a bunch of yelling and screaming coming through the interphone. I've been with the airline 26 years; I've never heard anything like that in my entire career." The captain then told the flight attendant, "We're landing the airplane now."

At the time of this decision, the aircraft was approximately 100 miles past Reno and 200 miles from Las Vegas. The plane was traveling at approximately 500 miles per hour, so the captain only had a few moments to make the decision whether to divert the plane to Reno or continue to Las Vegas. Captain Swanigan contacted air traffic control to report the disturbance and to request permission to make an emergency landing. He received permission and landed in Reno.

The aircraft was met at the gate by officers from the Reno police department. Captain Swanigan asked the flight attendants to assist the officers in securing the first-class cabin and then meet him at the top of the jetway to discuss what had happened.

According to the flight attendants, the Egyptians congregated near the cockpit, and when told that this was prohibited, they responded, "You Americans are so paranoid, and all of these safety and security regulations are stupid," and they refused to leave. After several admonitions, the flight attendants gave them a written warning, and they "exploded."

Captain Swanigan asked the police officers to remove the offending passengers and arrest them. After the plaintiffs were identified by the flight attendants, they were escorted off the plane. The plaintiffs were then led to an adjacent area, where the parties prepared written statements of the incident. The plaintiffs protested their innocence, but Captain Swanigan was adamant that the plaintiffs be arrested. The police ultimately decided that no crime had occurred, and they told the captain that the passengers would be released. But the captain refused to allow them to reboard the plane, so they took a flight on another airline.

Captain Swanigan and his crew returned to the aircraft and resumed the flight to Las Vegas. Back in the air, one of the flight attendants made a public announcement that the plaintiffs were responsible for the diversion. Following the incident, Alaska Airlines reported all nine passengers to the Joint Terrorism Task Force.

Because they had to take a later flight, the plaintiffs missed a scheduled meeting with the manufacturer of natural gas equipment that they had hoped to distribute in Egypt. The meeting was rescheduled, but that afternoon the plaintiffs were contacted by the FBI (no doubt responding to the terrorism report) and were marched under guard through the lobby of their hotel and questioned at length. According to the plaintiffs, they were interrogated about their Muslim faith, mosque affiliations, employment histories, and the incident on the airline. Mug shots were taken before they were released. As a consequence, they were two hours late for their meeting, and the transaction with the manufacturer was never completed. Word of the altercation made its way back to Egypt, where a U.S. State Department official mentioned it to one of the plaintiffs.

The plaintiffs sued Alaska Airlines, alleging damages under the Warsaw Convention and for a variety of state-law defamation and intentional infliction of emotional distress claims. The district court granted Alaska's motion for summary judgment on the Warsaw Convention claim on the ground that the airline was entitled to immunity under the treaty. The court also granted the airline's motion to dismiss the plaintiffs' state-law claims as being preempted by the Convention.

THE TOKYO CONVENTIONS

In the case of international flights, the common law is abrogated by treaty. Any claim by a passenger based on an airline's conduct during flight, or during the process of boarding or leaving the plane, is limited to damages provided by the treaty. This includes a passenger's claim that results from actions taken by the pilot or crew to preserve the order and safety on board the aircraft.

The Convention on Offenses and Certain Other Acts Committed on Board Aircraft, commonly called the Tokyo Convention, authorizes pilots to deplane passengers, to deliver passengers to law enforcement, and to forcibly restrain passengers during flight. Article 8 allows the captain to disembark anyone who he or she has reasonable grounds to believe has committed an act that "jeopardizes good order and discipline on board." Article 9 allows the captain to turn passengers over to the police if he or she has reasonable grounds to believe they have committed a "serious offense according to the penal law of the state of registration of the aircraft."

Alaska Airlines argued that it should not be held liable for its treatment of passengers under the Tokyo Convention unless Captain Swanigan acted in an "arbitrary and capricious" manner. But the court pointed out that the treaty and its drafting history say nothing about such standard. The standard the treaty adopts, the court said, is one of "reasonableness."

It is well settled that the interpretation of a treaty must begin with the language itself, and according to the court, the treaty clearly provides immunity to the airline only if the pilot has "reasonable grounds" to support his or her actions. The court also pointed out that the drafting history was entirely consistent with this plain language.

The court held that a fact finder could conclude that Captain Swanigan did not have reasonable grounds to believe that the plaintiffs posed a threat to the security of the aircraft. To begin with, the captain made the decision to divert the aircraft after one of the flight attendants reported that "she had lost control of the first-class cabin." The pilot asked no questions and did nothing else to confirm the flight attendant's statement. Neither he nor his copilot looked into the cabin through the cockpit window. In fact, after landing, Captain Swanigan told one of the flight attendants that he "had no idea what went on back there." A jury could conclude that a reasonable captain should have tried to find out *something* about what was happening in the cabin before making an emergency landing.

Captain Swanigan countered that he and the copilot heard shouting in the background when he spoke with the flight attendant. But this claim was contested by the plaintiffs and Ms. Shealy, who reported that the passengers had fallen silent by the time the flight attendant called the cockpit.

An expert witness for the plaintiffs stated in his declaration, "It is difficult to understand how Captain Swanigan could have allowed this event to escalate to the level that it did without ever asking anything about it. Actions taken in haste and without an understanding of the pertinent facts are unreasonable and in some cases even dangerous." A jury could have reasonably accepted this conclusion after hearing the evidence.

Even if the jury were to find that Captain Swanigan had reasonable grounds to divert the plane, the jury could well conclude that the pilot did not act reasonably once the plane was on the ground. At the time the captain landed the plane, he had no firsthand information about what had happened in the cabin. He ordered the plaintiffs deplaned based on his understanding at that time. Jurors could reasonably find that the captain should have listened to the plaintiffs' side of the story before turning them over to the police.

According to the airline, Captain Swanigan believed the plaintiffs' conduct violated the statute prohibiting interference with flight-crew members. But the court noted that the statute is violated *only* if the interference is accomplished by "assaulting or intimidating" a crew member. None of the passengers made threats or became physically aggressive with the flight attendants.

A jury could also conclude that even if Captain Swanigan initially had grounds to believe that the plaintiffs were disruptive, those grounds dissipated once the Reno police exonerated the plaintiffs and cleared them to continue flying. Further, when some of the plaintiffs asked Swanigan to let them reboard the airplane, he refused on the grounds that "his flight attendant would not allow it." Based on this evidence, a jury might well conclude that Captain Swanigan's refusal to let the plaintiffs continue on to their destination had nothing to do with safety but was designed to placate a flight attendant who had taken a dislike to certain passengers, perhaps because of their nationality or ethnicity.

Finally, the airline urged the court to affirm the district court on the ground that the captain must have broad discretion in preserving the safety of the plane and its passengers and must be able to rely on information he received from his crew when making those decisions. The appellate court agreed that the captain must be able to act decisively in an emergency, but a jury could reasonably conclude there was no emergency here. The court therefore reversed the summary judgment in favor of Alaska Airlines and remanded the case for these issues to be resolved at trial.

After the plane landed, Captain Swanigan and members of the crew gave formal statements about the incident to the Reno police. The plaintiffs claimed that these reports were knowingly or recklessly false and thus defamatory. The district court dismissed those claims pursuant to the Warsaw Convention, which preempted local law remedies for claims that occurred on board the aircraft or in the course of any of the operations of embarking or disembarking. The plaintiffs claimed that the Warsaw Convention did not apply because they had left the plane, and any actions by the airline fell outside the scope of the Convention.

The court pointed out that the statements were made in the gate area shortly after the plane landed. They were made for the purpose of transferring custody of the plaintiffs from the airlines to the police, as authorized by the Tokyo Convention. The Tokyo Convention, moreover, requires pilots to provide an explanation to local authorities when they transfer custody. The court found it fair to say that the pilot's statements to the police were part of the disembarkation process and covered by the Warsaw Convention. The appellate court therefore affirmed the district court's dismissal of the plaintiffs' defamation claims based on statements made in the terminal.

The plaintiffs further alleged that, after the flight left Reno for Las Vegas, a member of the crew made an in-flight announcement blaming the plaintiffs for causing the diversion. The plaintiffs argued that the Warsaw Convention's preemptive effect existed only so long as the passengers were still on the airplane, embarking onto the plane, or disembarking from the plane.

The district court dismissed this claim as preempted by the Warsaw Convention, but the appellate court noted that nothing in the language of the Convention suggested that it extended to lawsuits filed by passengers for occurrences *after* they disembarked. The court therefore reversed the district court's dismissal of plaintiffs' defamation claim for the in-flight announcement made after disembarkation.

The appellate court therefore concluded that substantial evidence supported the jury's finding that Captain Swanigan and his crew acted unreasonably toward the plaintiffs. The court reversed the grant of summary judgment in favor of the airline and remanded the case for trial along with the defamation claim for the in-flight announcement after the plane took off from Reno. The court affirmed the dismissal of plaintiffs' defamation claims for the statements made on the ground.

The dissent disagreed with the majority's adoption of a reasonableness standard, and it argued in favor of an "arbitrary or capricious" standard that gave

considerable deference to the pilot. Such broad immunity would, the dissent
argued, allow the pilot to act without hesitation to guard passenger safety and
to do so without concern of being second-guessed.

The dissent framed the gist of the controversy in these provocative, and very
memorable, words:

> Depending on whose perspective of the events one adopts, Cap-
> tain Swanigan, Alaska's vice president of flight operations, is either a
> dedicated, experienced pilot who believed that an in-flight emergency
> required him to immediately land his aircraft or a simpleton in charge
> of a cockpit crew that failed to follow airline procedures and who was
> buffaloed by two vindictive flight attendants into needlessly diverting the
> flight and forcing passengers off the plane. I take the former view.

12

+ + + + + + + + + + + + + + + + + + + +

FINAL JOURNEY
BREACHING THE TARIFF RULE

+ + + + + + + + + + + + + + + + + + + +

COUGHLIN V. TRANS WORLD AIRLINES
847 F.2d 1432 (9th Cir. 1988)

Most contents of checked luggage are of course easily replaceable—clothes, shoes, hair dryers, books, electronics. But Dorothy Coughlin's baggage, unfortunately, was not—it contained the cremated remains of her beloved husband. Mrs. Coughlin tried to carry the small box of ashes on board, but the agent refused to let her do so. (How the agent knew what was in the box is not known.) It also turns out that there was no prohibition against taking such in a carry-on bag.

Unfortunately, the checked luggage—along with the box containing Mr. Coughlin's remains—was lost by Trans World Airlines (TWA) and apparently never recovered. Which brings up the issue—where *does* all of this lost luggage end up?

In any event, Mrs. Coughlin sued TWA for $78,000, an amount exceeding the baggage liability limitation printed on her ticket, on the theory that the ticket agent's negligence in misinforming her that she was required to check the package—rather than taking it with her on the plane as she wished—voided the liability limitation.

TWA moved for summary judgment on the issue of whether the liability limitation was valid notwithstanding the airline's negligence. The district court granted the airline's motion, and in the subsequent trial, the court awarded Mrs. Coughlin the sum of $1,250—TWA's maximum liability under its tariff for the loss of baggage. Mrs. Coughlin appealed.

An air carrier may limit its liability for loss or destruction of luggage provided the carrier allows the passenger to protect her luggage by either carrying it on board or purchasing excess valuation insurance. These terms are interdependent: if the carrier is to limit its liability, it must allow alternative means of protecting the transported items. TWA's published tariff (a) limited its liability to $1,250 for loss or damage to baggage, (b) explained the procedure for purchasing extra insurance, and (c) expressly instructed passengers to carry their valuables personally.

The appellate court pointed out that TWA's ticket agent would not allow Mrs. Coughlin to carry her husband's cremated remains on board the aircraft, even though they were in a package well within the size restriction for carry-on luggage. The question was what effect the agent's actions had on the enforceability of the tariff limitation. The court concluded that by refusing to allow Mrs. Coughlin to carry the package on board, TWA breached Tariff Rule 230(B)(3), which provided that "valuables should be carried personally by the passenger."

The cremated remains of Mr. Coughlin were unquestionably valuable, and there was nothing in the record to suggest that they were prohibited. Under the express terms of the contract, Mrs. Coughlin should have been allowed to carry them on board. It is axiomatic that a material breach of an agreement warrants rescission. The courts have variously described the present situation as a failure or frustration of consideration, waiver, estoppel, and breach. Regardless of the term used, it was clear that TWA could not now attempt to enforce a provision of the contract it had violated. TWA's refusal to allow Mrs. Coughlin to protect her valuables by carrying them personally therefore denied her the benefit of the bargain with respect to the tariff agreement, and her case could then proceed.

But the nagging question of where poor Mr. Coughlin eventually landed remains unresolved.

13

+ + + + + + + + + + + + + + + + + + + +

STOLEN TICKETS
A DEFAMATION ACTION

+ + + + + + + + + + + + + + + + + + + +

TAJ MAHAL TRAVEL V. DELTA AIRLINES
164 F.3d 186 (3rd Cir. 1998)

Taj Mahal Travel was a travel agency based in Princeton, New Jersey, and it specialized in airline passage to India. Taj Mahal apparently purchased some of the tickets at issue from an agent for Delta Airlines and then in turn sold them to its clients.

On a number of occasions, these Taj Mahal tickets were presented at the airport in India for the return flight to the United States, and Delta refused to honor them. The passengers, who were forced to purchase new tickets, were given the following explanatory letter:

Dear Delta Customer:

We regretfully must inform you that the ticket presented has been reported as a stolen airline ticket.

It is unfortunate that you have purchased one of these tickets. While we empathize with your predicament, we cannot honor this ticket for transportation because Delta has not yet received the money you paid. To assist you in this difficult situation, we will sell you a new ticket, honoring the fare indicated in your flight reservation record and waiving any advance purchase requirements.

It is necessary to retain your ticket in order to assist with the ongoing law enforcement investigation; however, this letter will serve as your receipt for the ticket. If you purchased your ticket from an authorized Delta travel agency, please complete the attached affidavit and forward it to Delta Air Lines, Inc. for a refund. If you purchased the ticket from someone not authorized by Delta to sell its tickets, you should contact the individual from whom you purchased the ticket, as Delta has not received any payment for this ticket.

If this ticket has been issued by a travel agent and you have further questions, you may contact the Agency Audit and Fraud Prevention, Airline Reporting Corporation at (713) 816-8134.

In a complaint filed against the airline, Taj Mahal alleged that the letter was defamatory and caused its patrons not only to demand reimbursement, but also to cease doing business with the agency. Claiming injury to its reputation and its business, Taj Mahal sought compensatory and punitive damages.

The district court entered judgment for Delta, holding that the letter could not be reasonably interpreted to have a defamatory meaning. The court further held that even if the letter was defamatory, Taj Mahal failed to show that the statements were "of and concerning" the plaintiff. According to the court, the letter did not mention the plaintiff by name and did not specify by name or implication any particular person or entity. Rather, it referred to any number of travel agents without reference to any particular one.

Taj Mahal appealed the ruling, contending that a reasonable reader could understand the letters to accuse the agency of selling tickets for which it had not paid. It also asserted that actions for defamation were not preempted by the Airline Deregulation Act (ADA).

THE DEFAMATION ISSUE

To state a claim for defamation in New Jersey, the plaintiff must prove (1) that the defendant made a defamatory statement of fact, (2) concerning the plaintiff,

(3) which was false, (4) which was communicated to persons other than the plaintiff, and (5) fault. Not only must the statement be defamatory, it must also be "of and concerning" the plaintiff. A defamatory statement need not explicitly name a plaintiff, so long as it was reasonably understood to refer to the plaintiff by at least one third party.

The letter at issue stated that (a) "the ticket presented has been reported as . . . stolen," (b) "it is unfortunate that you have purchased one of these tickets," and (c) "Delta has not yet received the money you paid." The appellate court held that the letter thus linked theft (a criminal offense) to the ticket received from Taj Mahal. In addition, the letter indicated, "It is necessary to retain your ticket in order to assist with the ongoing law enforcement investigation." Clearly, the appellate court concluded, this statement emphasized that some type of criminal misappropriation was involved. The court concluded that the text at hand permitted an inference of defamatory meaning.

The issue remained whether the letter would lead a reasonable reader to conclude that Taj Mahal was in some way connected with the purported illegality. The appellate court believed that it could. To begin with, the client knew that he paid Taj Mahal. The Delta letter noted that the reason for refusal to "honor this ticket for transportation [is] because Delta has not yet received the money you paid." Yet Taj Mahal was the *only* entity with which the client had contact. The court found it reasonable to infer that if Delta did not receive that money, then Taj Mahal did not transmit the payment. The final sentence of the letter strengthened this assumption: "If this ticket has been issued by a travel agent and you have further questions, you may contact the Agency Audit and Fraud Prevention, Airline Reporting Corporation."

Delta contended that the letter could refer to any number of travel agents or other intermediaries. But the recipient of the letter did not buy his ticket from any number of travel agents, the court said—he bought it from Taj Mahal. The imputation of fraud and dishonesty focused on the agency from which the passenger purchased the ticket. The average airline passenger was unlikely to know of any intermediaries between the travel agency and the airline.

It was possible, the appellate court pointed out, that a fact finder might conceivably adopt Delta's contention that the letter did not point to Taj Mahal. However, at this stage of the litigation, the court refused to resolve this ambiguity against the plaintiff. The court concluded, therefore, that the letter was capable of defamatory meaning directed at Taj Mahal and that the district court erred in entering judgment for the airline.

THE PREEMPTION ISSUE

Applying the foregoing considerations, the appellate court held that the plaintiff's defamation claims were not preempted and could therefore proceed. Application of state law in these circumstances did not frustrate congressional intent, nor did it impose a state utility-like regulation on the airlines. Therefore, the plaintiff's suit was simply "too tenuous, remote, or peripheral" to be subject to preemption, even though Delta's statements did refer to ticketing, which is arguably a "service."

Taj Mahal also asserted a claim for punitive damages. The district court reasoned that such an award might be preempted, provided it related to airline "rates, routes, or services." However, the appellate court was not persuaded by that reasoning, because defamation is so foreign to regulations on prices, routes, and services that it was unlikely that an award of traditional damages would offend congressional intent. Punitive damages have long been a part of traditional state tort law, and it was the airline's burden to show that Congress intended to preclude such awards. Because defamation claims were not preempted, the appellate court concluded that customary remedies, including punitive damages, survived as well. Accordingly, the appellate court reversed the judgment of the district court and remanded the case for further proceedings.

A dissent to the majority opinion agreed that the ADA did not preempt the litigation, but it concluded that the letter sent by Delta could not reasonably be deemed defamatory. In the view of the dissent, the preliminary question was whether the words were capable of a defamatory meaning. Courts should give the statement its "fair and natural" meaning that a person of ordinary intelligence and sensibility would give it.

The dissent felt that the Delta letter did not rise to the level of attributing criminal conduct to Taj Mahal. The letter merely stated that the passenger's ticket was "reported" as stolen and that there was an "ongoing law enforcement investigation" under way. An indispensable prerequisite for a defamation action is that the alleged defamatory statement be "of and concerning" the plaintiff, and a party claiming to have been defamed must show that the statement referred specifically to it. Because the Delta letter did not satisfy the threshold standard, the dissent maintained that it could not, as a matter of law, be considered defamatory.

14

+ + + + + + + + + + + + + + + + + + +

HIJACKED!
THE JURISDICTIONAL HURDLES

+ + + + + + + + + + + + + + + + + + +

PFLUG V. EGYPTAIR CORP.
961 F.2d 26 (2nd Cir. 1992)

Jackie Pflug purchased a round-trip ticket in Athens for a flight to Cairo on Egyptair, the national airline. During her return trip on November 23, 1985, terrorists took control of Flight 648 and forced the pilot to land on the Island of Malta.

While the aircraft was on the ground, the hijackers collected the American and Israeli passengers and began executing them. They forced Mrs. Pflug to exit the aircraft and shot her in the head while she was standing on a set of stairs next to the aircraft door. She fell to the ground and lay there unattended, feigning death. Five hours later, employees of Egyptair removed her. Discovering that she was alive, they sent her to the hospital.

When she recovered, Pflug, a resident of Minnesota, brought an action for personal injuries against a wholly owned subsidiary of Egyptair called Egyptair Corporation, which was incorporated in New York. Her complaint alleged that jurisdiction existed in the district court under the terms of the Warsaw Convention and under the court's diversity jurisdiction.

In its answer, Egyptair Corporation admitted that it owned and operated the hijacked aircraft but denied that it was incorporated and domiciled in New York. Six months later, counsel for Egyptair Corporation submitted that the admission and denial were mistakes resulting from (a) counsel's ignorance of the existence of the subsidiary "paper" New York corporation and (b) his assumption that the party being sued was Egyptair, the Egyptian national airline.

Egyptair Corporation then moved to dismiss the complaint for lack of subject matter jurisdiction on the grounds that the United States did not qualify as a permissible forum under the Warsaw Convention and, alternatively, for summary judgment on the ground that Egyptair Corporation was not a carrier and did not operate the hijacked aircraft.

The judge granted the motion to dismiss for lack of subject matter jurisdiction. The court found that the Warsaw Convention applied to all causes of action asserted in the complaint and that the provision of the Convention allowing the plaintiff to sue in the domicile of the carrier did not allow jurisdiction in the United States because the carrier was domiciled in Egypt.

THE WARSAW CONVENTION

Suits by passengers injured in international air travel are exclusively governed by the Warsaw Convention, a treaty creating an absolute right to compensation for passengers but at the same time imposing a liability limit. The Convention set limitations on who may be sued by an injured passenger and where suit may be brought. Unless an action is brought in accordance with these limitations, the federal courts lack treaty jurisdiction under the Convention, as well as jurisdiction over the subject matter if the suit fails. The Second Circuit had previously held that when an action is one that falls within the province of the Convention, and the Convention does not authorize suit in the jurisdiction in which the action is brought, the court's inquiry ceases without an examination of diversity jurisdiction. Thus, as an initial matter the court in the present case had to determine whether the Convention applied to all of the plaintiffs' claims.

Article 17 of the Convention provides that:

> The carrier shall be liable for damage sustained in the event of the death or wounding of a passenger or any other bodily injury suffered by a passenger, if the accident which caused the damage so sustained took place on board the aircraft or in the course of any of the operations of embarking or disembarking.

Pflug argued that the district court should not have dismissed her complaint because the Convention only applied to "accidents," and hijacking did not necessarily constitute an accident for purposes of the Convention. She claimed that the district court should have submitted the question of whether her injuries resulted from an "accident" to the trier of fact. She further claimed that at least some of her causes of action fell outside Article 17 in that they sought recovery for injuries that did not occur while she was on the aircraft. The court found these arguments unpersuasive. The court therefore concluded that a hijacking clearly qualifies as an accident under Article 17.

Mrs. Pflug claimed that her injuries occurred on the tarmac and therefore did not take place "on board the aircraft," but the court found that fact irrelevant. Article 17 applied if the *accident* occurred in the aircraft. It did not put any limitation on where the injuries could have occurred. The "accident" at issue was the hijacking, and that event took place on board the aircraft.

THE CARRIER QUESTION

Article 17 states that "the carrier shall be liable" to injured passengers. The question in this case was whether Egyptair Corporation was a "carrier" involved in the occurrences at issue. This question was obviously antecedent to an examination of whether the United States was one of the jurisdictions in which Article 28 (the forum-limiting provision of the Convention) allowed the plaintiffs to proceed against the carrier.

Article 28 states that:

(1) An action for damages must be brought, at the option of the plaintiff, in the territory of one of the High Contracting Parties, either before the court of the *domicile* of the carrier or of his *principal place of business,* or where he has a *place of business through which the contract has been made,* or before the court at the *place of destination.*

(2) Questions of procedure shall be governed by the law of the court to which the case is submitted.

Pflug did not dispute that Egypt was the carrier's principal place of business, its domicile, and the place of destination of the flight and that Athens was the location where the contract was made with the plaintiff. However, she argued that the district judge erred in holding that the carrier did not also have a domicile in the United States. Pflug claimed that the defendant's domicile was

491

in New York. But as the court pointed out, the defendant was not the carrier, and the carrier was not named as a defendant.

Pflug attempted to assert that Egyptair Corporation was not a separate corporation from Egyptair, the national airline of Egypt. She argued that Egyptair and Egyptair Corporation were a single corporation and that corporation was clearly the airline that operated Flight 648. She claimed that Egyptair in effect reincorporated itself in the United States by organizing a subsidiary corporation and thus had two places of incorporation. She argued that the district court erred in dismissing the case because the Convention did not preclude multiple domiciles.

However, the district court found that Egyptair and Egyptair Corporation were two separate corporations. Egyptair is the national airline of Egypt, and it existed for almost 20 years before the incorporation of Egyptair Corporation. The two corporations had different principal places of business: Egyptair's principal place of business was Egypt, while Egyptair Corporation's certificate of incorporation was New York.

The appellate court noted that Egyptair was not reincorporated in New York and that Egyptair Corporation was not the old corporation but separately incorporated. Therefore, Egyptair and Egyptair Corporation were two distinct corporations, not one corporation incorporated in both Egypt and the United States. Egyptair's domicile in Egypt was never moved. Additionally, the evidence unequivocally proved that Egyptair Corporation was not a carrier and did not engage to transport the plaintiff. In fact, Egyptair Corporation did not own or operate any aircraft, did not own any assets, did not have any employees, and did not even have a CAB permit to operate aircraft. The plaintiff did business with Egyptair, the national airline of Egypt, not Egyptair Corporation, its subsidiary.

According to the terms of the Warsaw Convention, injured passengers have a cause of action against the airline that is "the carrier" involved in the accident. Cases interpreting Article 17 and other articles of the Convention have established that only the airline that actually transports the injured passenger can be held liable as "the carrier."

Because Mrs. Pflug brought suit against a corporation that was not the carrier that transported her on the hijacked flight, the district court properly dismissed her claims for lack of subject-matter jurisdiction.

15

+ + + + + + + + + + + + + + + + + + + +

CRAMPED SEATS
A CAUSE OF ACTION?

+ + + + + + + + + + + + + + + + + + + +

WITTY V. DELTA AIR LINES
366 F.3d 380 (5th Cir. 2004)

No one has ever seriously argued that seats located in the coach section of an aircraft are comfortable. Milton Witty brought suit against Delta Air Lines claiming that the seating of the airline was so bad he developed deep vein thrombosis (DVT) while on a flight from Monroe, Louisiana, to Hartford, Connecticut.

DVT occurs when a blood clot develops in a deep vein, usually in the leg. It can cause serious complications if the clot breaks off and travels to the lungs or brain. Witty alleged that Delta was negligent in failing to warn passengers about the risks of DVT. He asserted that the warning should be "that there is a high risk of developing DVT in pressurized cabins that exceed a certain length of time." He also complained that Delta was negligent (a) in failing to provide adequate legroom to prevent DVT and (b) in failing to allow passengers to exercise their legs.

Delta filed a motion to dismiss, arguing that the state-law claims were pre-empted. The district court denied the motion, reasoning that state regulation of airline "services" *was* preempted, but that state tort actions for personal physical injuries caused by the operation and maintenance of aircraft were not. The court concluded that Witty's claim arose from the operation of Delta's aircraft and therefore was not preempted.

The Fifth Circuit saw things a little differently. It explained that the Airline Deregulation Act (ADA) not only preempted the direct regulation of prices by states, but that it also preempted indirect regulation "relating to" prices that has a "forbidden significant effect" on such prices. While the state regulation of legroom might not relate to prices as obviously as the state regulation of, say, fare advertising, the economic effect on prices would still be significant, the court said. The plaintiff's failure-to-warn claim presented a closer question, but the court concluded that under the implied preemption doctrine, Congress also intended to preempt state standards for the warnings that must be given airline passengers.

The court explained that the express preemption provision of the ADA was not the only conceivable basis for finding preemption in a personal injury case based on inadequate safety warnings. There was a separate federal act, the Federal Aviation Act, that addressed air safety. The act not only authorized but affirmatively directed its administrator to promulgate air safety standards and regulations, including standards and regulations relating to aircraft design, maintenance, and inspection. A state claim is preempted where congressional intent to preempt is inferred from the existence of a pervasive regulatory scheme or where state law conflicts with federal law or the achievement of federal objectives. In the instant case, the court found that field preemption and conflict preemption were both applicable, because there existed a comprehensive scheme of federal regulation, and the imposition of state standards would conflict with federal law and its objectives.

The appellate court held that federal regulatory requirements for passenger safety warnings and instructions were exclusive and therefore preempted all state standards and requirements. Congress enacted a pervasive regulatory scheme covering air safety, and the interdependence of these factors requires a uniform and exclusive system of federal regulation if the congressional objectives underlying the Federal Aviation Act were to be fulfilled. In this case, the conflict was more than theoretical, because Witty claimed that a DVT warning should have been given, even though federal regulations did not require such a warning. Any warning that passengers should not stay in their seats but should instead move about to prevent DVT would necessarily conflict with any federal determination that, all things considered, passengers are safer in their seats.

The court therefore concluded that the legroom claim was preempted by the ADA and that federal law exclusively provided the safety warnings that airlines must provide to passengers. Because there was no federal requirement that airlines give DVT warnings, Witty's state claim for failure to warn failed.

And future passengers, it appeared, would be forced to remain in their very small—and very uncomfortable—seats.

16

+ + + + + + + + + + + + + + + + + + +

CLAIM CHECK
STRICTLY BY THE BOOK

+ + + + + + + + + + + + + + + + + + +

SPANNER V. UNITED AIRLINES
177 F.3d 1173 (9th Cir. 1999)

Robert Spanner and his wife returned to San Francisco International Airport after a two-week trip to New Zealand. The Spanners had traveled on Air New Zealand between Auckland and Los Angeles. It turned out their claim checks were "defective"—they did not contain (a) the ticket number, (b) the number and weight of their bags, or (c) a statement that their travel was subject to the rules of the Warsaw Convention.

At Los Angeles International Airport, the Spanners deplaned, took possession of their luggage, cleared customs, and then checked their luggage on a United Airlines flight to San Francisco. Although the claim checks for the luggage were the same as those issued by Air New Zealand, the Spanners also received from United a ticket called a Plane Ticket and Baggage Check (PTBC).

The PTBC contained a complete statement of the limited liability provisions of the Warsaw Convention. United alleged that a handwritten notation of the weight and number of the checked bags typically would appear on the PTBC or on the boarding pass.

The Spanners pointed out that some or all of this documentation was taken when they boarded the plane. The district court found it impossible to determine whether any notation of the weight or number of the Spanners' bags was ever made on either their PTBC or their boarding pass. No such notation was made on the Air New Zealand claim checks.

When the Spanners arrived in San Francisco, they could not find their luggage on the baggage carousel. A clerk informed them that their bags had arrived on an earlier United flight, and he directed them to a cluster of bags in the baggage terminal. There the Spanners were able to find three of their four bags. The clerk checked his computer and informed the Spanners that all four bags had indeed arrived. United searched for the missing bag for several weeks without success. The Spanners subsequently filed a claim for approximately $8,500 (they eventually sued for slightly more than $7,400), the alleged value of the lost bag and its contents. (Query: What exactly did they have in those bags?) In any event, United refused to reimburse the claimed amount.

The Spanners filed suit, and United claimed that its liability was governed by the Warsaw Convention and was therefore limited to $9.07 per pound of lost luggage. The Spanners contended that United could not limit its liability because United had failed to issue the Spanners a proper baggage check indicating the weight and number of bags. The Spanners and United both moved for summary judgment.

The district court granted United's motion for summary judgment. It was undisputed, based on an examination of an exemplar passenger ticket, that United had provided the Spanners with notice of the liability limitations under the Convention. But the court held that United failed to show that it had noted on the baggage check the weight and number of the Spanners' bags. The court nonetheless concluded that United could avail itself of limited liability, because a technical failure to comply with the Warsaw Convention does not preclude liability limitations that do not prejudice the claimants.

Because the Spanners were given notice of the Warsaw Convention, and because United had agreed to pay the Spanners as if their bag had weighed the maximum permitted (70 pounds), the district court concluded that the Spanners had not been prejudiced by the failure to note the weight and number of bags. The district court granted United summary judgment for limited liability based on an assumed weight of 70 pounds, or $634.90. The Spanners, naturally, appealed.

CARGO LIABILITY

The Warsaw Convention was drafted at international conferences in Paris in 1925 and Warsaw in 1929. The United States became a signatory in 1934. More than 120 nations have since signed the treaty. A central quid pro quo of the Convention is presumptive liability for the loss of cargo (Article 18) but a modest limit on carrier liability calculated by the weight of the cargo (Article 22). In order to invoke the limited liability of the Convention, a carrier must meet several requirements. Among them are that the loss must occur during "international transportation" (Article 1) and that any transportation of baggage must include a baggage check given to the passenger that includes certain items of information (Article 4).

The parties agreed that the Spanners' bags were lost during international transportation, even though the loss was during a shuttle from Los Angeles to San Francisco. Article 1(1) of the Warsaw Convention defines "international transportation" as transportation between "two High Contracting Parties," and the United States and New Zealand were both High Contracting Parties. The Spanners' flight from Los Angeles to San Francisco was still part of this "international transportation" because, under Article 1(3), transportation to be performed by several successive air carriers is deemed to be one undivided transportation. Article 1(3) provides further that transportation "shall not lose its international character merely because one contract or a series of contracts is to be performed entirely within a territory subject to one High Contracting Party."

Article 4(1) requires the carrier to deliver a baggage check, and Article 4(3)(f) provides that the baggage check must contain the "number and weight of the packages." If a carrier fails to deliver such a baggage check, Article 4(4) sternly says that "the carrier shall not be entitled to avail itself of those provisions of the convention which exclude or limit its liability."

The appellate court reasoned that United simply could not overcome the clear text of Article 4. A baggage check "shall contain" a notation of the weight and number of bags, and when this specific requirement is not met, a carrier "shall not" be entitled to avail itself of limited liability.

After much analysis, the court reversed the summary judgment in favor of United Airlines—and all because of a poorly prepared claim check.

17

+ +

PLANE CHANGE
ASSERTING PUNITIVE DAMAGES

+ +

WEST V. NORTHWEST AIRLINES
995 F.2d 148 (9th Cir. 1993)

William West purchased a non-refundable, non-changeable ticket to travel on Northwest Airlines from Great Falls, Montana, to Arlington, Virginia. Between the date of purchase and the scheduled departure date, Northwest decided to reduce the size of its aircraft from a Boeing 727 (which accommodates 146 passengers) to a DC 9 (which holds only 78 people).

When West arrived at the gate, a Northwest employee informed him that the flight was overbooked. Northwest attempted to make room for West and other passengers by requesting volunteers to relinquish their seats in exchange for a voucher. However, only three people accepted, and West was unable to board the flight.

Northwest then offered West an alternate flight that would arrive at nearby Dulles Airport at 3:00 a.m. the next morning. West declined and made his own arrangements to travel to Arlington at a later date. West filed claims in state court for breach of the covenant of good faith and fair dealing under Montana law and for unjust discrimination under the Federal Aviation Act, seeking both compensatory and punitive damages on the state and federal claims.

Northwest moved for summary judgment on the grounds that the period for bringing a claim had expired, and that West's state claim was in any event preempted by the FAA. The district court granted Northwest's motion for summary judgment on both grounds.

West appealed only the preemption issue.

PREEMPTION ANALYSIS

The Ninth Circuit looked closely at the U.S. Supreme Court decision in *Morales v. Trans World Airlines*. In that case, the court considered whether or not the Airline Deregulation Act (ADA) preempted enforcement of consumer protection laws that in effect regulated air fare advertising. The court held that the ADA expressly preempted these guidelines because their enforcement related to "rates, routes, or services" of an air carrier. In crafting this clause, reasoned the court, Congress intended to preempt state laws that interfered with the goal of deregulating the airline industry. *Morales* did leave open the possibility that certain state laws would not be preempted by the ADA because they were "too tenuous, remote, or peripheral" to have a preemptive effect.

The Ninth Circuit concluded that the ADA did not preempt West's claim for compensatory damages under state law, but that it did preempt his claim for punitive damages. The court reasoned that the state contract and tort laws under which West sought relief were within that range of statutes too tenuously connected to airline regulation to trigger preemption under the ADA—what *Morales* called "borderline questions." *Morales* unfortunately did not provide much guidance on which state laws fell into this category and which did not. The Supreme Court noted that if Congress has explicitly left a gap for the agency to fill, there is an express delegation of authority to the agency to elucidate a specific provision of the statute by regulation. Such legislative regulations are given controlling weight unless they are arbitrary, capricious, or manifestly contrary to the statute. In the case of the ADA, the agency regulations interpreting the Federal Aviation Act (Aviation Act) are particularly illuminating.

Part 250 of Title 14 of the Code of Federal Regulations contains a detailed set of rules pertaining to overbooking of flights. In the wake of the deregulation legislation, Part 250 was substantially amended, but Section 250.9, the provision giving passengers the option of rejecting airline compensation and pursuing a remedy under state law, was not altered. This provision expressly contemplates that an injured passenger may seek relief in court for being bumped from an

overbooked flight. According to Section 250.9(b), the bumped passenger has
three options: (1) he may accept the airline's offer of alternate transportation,
(2) he may accept airline compensation (in the form of money or a voucher for
future travel or some combination of the two), or (3) he may decline the payment and seek to recover damages in a court of law.

The Ninth Circuit and at least one other circuit had previously recognized
the controlling authority of this provision in the post-deregulation period,
holding that a passenger involuntarily denied boarding could not seek a state
tort remedy under Section 250.9(b) because she had already accepted the airline's offer of alternate transportation. The court reasoned that were it to hold
that West's state claims were preempted completely by the ADA, it would
eviscerate the third option.

Overbooking is an accepted form of price competition and reduction in the
deregulation period, and thus any law or regulation that results in penalizing
airlines for these practices is preempted by the Aviation Act. However, West's
right to pursue *punitive* damages in his state claims was limited because those
damages by their very nature, the court reasoned, seek to punish the entity
against whom they are awarded. Such damages would be contrary to the goals
of deregulation.

For the foregoing reasons, the court found that while West's state claim for
punitive damages was preempted by the Aviation Act, his claim for compensatory damages was not.

18

+ +

CHECKING CONTRABAND
AN UNAUTHORIZED SEARCH?

+ +

UNITED STATES V. GOMEZ
614 F.2d 643 (9th Cir. 1979)

Drug smugglers using checked baggage to transport their illegal wares might be best advised to at least use a sturdy identification tag. Just ask Angela Luz Gomez, who was tried for violating the narcotics laws after the court denied her motion to suppress evidence.

The story begins with a Dade County detective assigned to Miami International Airport. On the evening of March 31, 1979, he saw a suitcase that appeared to have fallen from a National Airlines conveyor belt. The bag bore no identification. The detective notified the airline's shift supervisor, who in turn made inquiries at the ticket counter. When no one could identify the suitcase, the supervisor took it to an office, accompanied by the detective who found it. The supervisor tried to open the suitcase to determine the identity of the owner, but when he could not unlock it, the officer kicked it open with the back of his shoe.

The supervisor lifted the lid of the suitcase, and inside was a revolver and several small packages wrapped in opaque plastic. The supervisor promptly turned the suitcase over to the police, and their search disclosed that the packages contained 23 pounds of 70 percent cocaine, having a street value in the millions of dollars. Nothing in the interior of the suitcase indicated who the owner was. But coincidentally enough, Ms. Gomez reported a lost suitcase which matched the description of the one with the cocaine inside, and when the airline delivered the bag to her in Los Angeles, she was arrested.

The district judge found that the suitcase was opened by the airline employee for the purpose of determining its ownership. The officer testified that he never suggested opening it and that it would be improper for him to make such a suggestion. The shift supervisor testified that the decision to open the suitcase was his alone. He stated that he was simply trying to reunite the lost luggage with its owner, and that opening the suitcase was necessary to do so.

The law is clear that a carrier's search, on its own initiative and for its own purposes, is a private (and not a governmental) search, and thus does not give rise to Fourth Amendment protections. The court noted that there was nothing unreasonable about a carrier opening luggage that had no identification in order to locate the owner. A search by airline personnel of luggage left at an airport is clearly a private search.

The evidence in the present case supported the district judge's finding that the decision to initiate the search was that of the airline employee. Gomez suggested that the search became a governmental one due to the presence of the officers and their observation of the airline employee's actions. The court soundly rejected this contention.

The appellate court noted that this case was somewhat more complicated because there was more than mere observation by the officers. The officer tapped the lock of the suitcase and thus assisted the airline employee in opening the bag. The officer, the court noted, was present out of an interest in helping the airline, and he was admittedly curious. The record contained absolutely no evidence that he suspected that the suitcase contained contraband. The court was therefore not inclined to hold that his presence and conduct constituted the search a governmental one, such as to bring into play the exclusionary rule.

The court did not accept Gomez's analogy of this case to that in *Corngold v. United States,* where FBI agents asked the airline employee to open a box and then assisted in holding back the flaps as he did so, or *United States v. Chadwick,* which involved the governmental search of a footlocker made shortly after the arrest of the owner. These cases were directed *to* a police search of a suitcase of someone who was identified in advance as a suspect. This was obviously not the situation here.

The moral of the case was clear: if you're going to smuggle drugs in checked luggage, you should make doubly sure that your name is on the outside of the bag.

19

+ +

PRECIOUS CARGO
A MATTER OF CONTRACT

+ +

DEIRO V. AMERICAN AIRLINES
816 F.2d 1360 (9th Cir. 1987)

Thomas Deiro filed this action against American Airlines for breach of contract, negligence, and willful and wanton behavior. He alleged damages of approximately $900,000 for the death of seven greyhound racing dogs and injuries to two others on a flight from Portland, Oregon, to Boston, with a stop and change of aircraft in Dallas/Fort Worth.

Deiro alleged that during the layover in Dallas/Fort Worth, the dogs were placed in a baggage cart on the tarmac, which was exposed to the hot sun in 100-degree temperatures without proper ventilation or water. The complaint also alleged that, despite Deiro's warnings to American personnel, the dogs were never attended to by the airline and that Deiro was not allowed to care for the dogs himself. When the flight arrived in Boston, an autopsy revealed that the dogs died from heat exposure.

The district court held that American's liability was limited to $750 as expressly set forth in his passenger ticket. Deiro filed an appeal, which reviewed three issues: (1) whether the contract of carriage contractually bound

Deiro to the $750 limitation, (2) whether American gave him reasonable notice and a full and fair opportunity to declare a higher value for his baggage and obtain greater protection, and (3) whether a common carrier can contractually limit its liability for gross negligence.

After he made his reservations, Deiro received a ticket coupon that contained the following provision:

> Liability for loss, delay, or damage to baggage is limited as follows unless a higher value is declared in advance and additional charges are paid: For travel wholly between U.S. points, to $750 per passenger. Excess valuation may not be declared on certain types of valuable articles. Carriers assume no liability for fragile or perishable articles. Further information may be obtained from the carrier.

Deiro never asked about declaring a higher value for the dogs, and he was not informed of this option by any airline personnel. The face of the baggage ticket stated in small print: "BAGGAGE CHECKED SUBJECT TO TARIFFS, INCLUDING LIMITATIONS OF LIABILITY THEREIN CONTAINED."

FINE-PRINT LIABILITY LIMITATIONS

To determine an airline's liability, courts examine the entire airline ticket in order to answer the pertinent question: Does the contract reasonably communicate to the passenger the existence of important terms and conditions that affect the passenger's legal rights? Most courts use a "reasonable communicativeness" test to determine when the passenger is contractually bound by the fine print of a ticket.

To determine reasonable communicativeness, the courts have typically employed a two-pronged analysis. First, the physical characteristics of the ticket—size of type, conspicuousness and clarity of notice on the face of the ticket, and the ease with which a passenger can read the provisions in question—are examined. Second, the circumstances surrounding the passenger's purchase of the ticket may be of equal importance. These surrounding circumstances include the passenger's familiarity with the ticket, the time and incentive to study the provisions of the ticket, and any other notice that the passenger received apart from the ticket.

The court in the present case noted that if the only consideration were the physical characteristics of the ticket, this would be a close call. The instant case fell between those cases in which notice on the face of the ticket was virtually nonexistent and those in which it was clear and conspicuous. Even relative to the small size of the face of the ticket, the type size of the message "SUBJECT TO CONDITIONS CONTAINED IN THIS TICKET" was tiny and not highlighted by a different-colored background. It was doubtful that this line alone could constitute a reasonable effort by the airline to provide a "clear and conspicuous" notice to its passengers that important conditions of carriage were contained inside the ticket coupon.

On the other hand, a warning was located at the top of the ticket in the far-left corner. The message to be conveyed by the notice was clear. Additionally, the notices contained inside the ticket coupon were conspicuous, especially the notice in relatively large type under the sizeable heading "NOTICE OF BAGGAGE LIABILITY LIMITATIONS."

What was a close call became decidedly clear when one considered the extrinsic factors which indicated the passenger's ability to become informed of the contractual terms at stake. It was undisputed that Deiro was an experienced air traveler who flew six to ten times a year. It was also undisputed that he knew there was "a whole bunch of stuff printed on the back of the ticket." That he "did not read all of that" only reinforced his knowledge of the ticket's written provisions.

It was also undisputed that the ticket was delivered to Deiro nine days before his flight. Therefore, he had ample opportunity to become familiar with the baggage liability limitations, especially when he knew in advance that he would be shipping valuable cargo.

RELEASED VALUATION DOCTRINE

Under the federal common law, common carriers may partially limit their liability for injury, loss, or destruction of baggage on a "released valuation" basis. Under this doctrine, in exchange for a low carriage rate, the shipper is deemed to have released the carrier from liability beyond a stated amount.

The carrier can lawfully limit recovery to an amount less than the actual loss if it provides a fair opportunity for the shipper to choose higher liability by paying an additional charge. Therefore, the shipper is bound only if he has reasonable notice of the rate structure and is given a fair opportunity to pay a higher rate in order to obtain greater protection.

The court noted that the federal common law applicable to carriers was not altered with the regulation of air carriers. The subsequent deregulation of air carriers in 1978 did not change the substantive content of the relevant federal common law. In the instant case, the court found that the airline provided Deiro with a full opportunity to declare a higher value for his dogs and therefore receive greater protection against loss.

GROSS NEGLIGENCE

Deiro contended that even if the liability limitation had legal effect, it could not shield the airline from its own gross negligence. The case law, said the court, was decidedly to the contrary. Under the federal common law, only an *appropriation* of property by the carrier for its own use will vitiate limits on liability. Consequently, if a liability limitation is valid, a passenger's recovery for damage cannot exceed the released value, regardless of the carrier's negligence.

The appellate court therefore concluded that Deiro was contractually bound to the $750 limitation, as harsh as that result seems to pet lovers everywhere.

20

+ + + + + + + + + + + + + + + + + + + +

FOOD AND WATER
A FEDERAL CONCERN

+ + + + + + + + + + + + + + + + + + + +

AIR TRANSPORT V. CUOMO
520 F.3d 218 (2nd Cir. 2008)

After a series of well-publicized incidents during the winter of 2007 in which airline passengers endured lengthy delays while grounded on New York runways, the New York legislature decided to do something. It enacted the Passenger Bill of Rights (PBR), which provided as follows:

Whenever airline passengers have boarded an aircraft and are delayed more than three hours on the aircraft prior to takeoff, the carrier shall ensure that passengers are provided as needed with:

(a) electric generation service to provide temporary power for fresh air and lights;
(b) waste removal service in order to service the holding tanks for on-board restrooms; and
(c) adequate food and drinking water and other refreshments.

The law also required all carriers to prominently display contact information for consumer complaints and an explanation of these rights. (Regulations adopted by the federal Department of Transportation in 2011 require airlines to provide food, water, and working lavatories during any tarmac delay of more than two hours.)

The Air Transport Association (ATA), the principal trade and service organization of the airline industry, filed suit seeking declaratory and injunctive relief on the grounds that the PBR was preempted by the Airline Deregulation Act (ADA) and thus violated the Commerce Clause of the U.S. Constitution.

The district court granted summary judgment to the state, holding that the PBR was not expressly preempted by the ADA because it was unrelated to a "price, route, or service of an air carrier," and was not impliedly preempted because Congress did not intend for the ADA to occupy the field of airplane safety.

ATA promptly appealed the ruling.

SUPREMACY CLAUSE

ATA asserted its claim under the Supremacy Clause, claiming that the provisions of the PBR violated the ADA. The Second Circuit explained that a preemption claim under the Supremacy Clause is distinct from a claim for enforcement of a federal law. A claim under the Supremacy Clause simply asserts that a federal statute has taken away local authority to regulate a certain activity. A private right of action, on the other hand, is a means of enforcing the substantive provisions of a federal law, and it provides remedies for violations of federal law by a government entity or a private party. The fact that the federal law in question in this case contained its own preemption language did not affect this distinction.

The court explained that Congress enacted the ADA to reduce economic regulation of the airline industry after it determined that competitive market forces would best further efficiency, innovation, and low prices, as well as variety and quality of air transportation. To ensure that the states would not enact regulation of their own, Congress included an express preemption provision. Recognizing this goal, the U.S. Supreme Court has repeatedly emphasized the breadth of the ADA's preemption provision.

Although the Second Circuit had not yet defined "service" as it was used in the ADA, it had little difficulty concluding that requiring airlines to provide food, water, electricity, and restrooms to passengers during lengthy ground delays related to the "service" of an air carrier. A majority of the circuits have held that the term "service" encompasses a broad range of matters, such as boarding procedures, baggage handling, and food and drink—matters incidental to and distinct from the actual transportation of passengers. The Third and Ninth Circuits, in contrast, have construed service to refer more narrowly to "the prices, schedules, origins and destinations of the point-to-point transportation of passengers, cargo, or mail," but *not* to include "an airline's provision of in-flight beverages, personal assistance to passengers, the handling of luggage, and similar amenities."

In the present case, the Second Circuit held that if "service" did not extend beyond prices, schedules, origins, and destinations, and that if federal preemption did not reach such regulation, a patchwork of state laws, rules, and regulations would result, and would therefore conflict with Congress's effort to leave such decisions to the competitive marketplace. In effect, the court said, the PBR substituted New York's priorities for competitive market forces, requiring airlines to provide services that New York specified. The court concluded that requiring airlines to provide food, water, electricity, and restrooms to passengers during lengthy ground delays did relate to the service of an air carrier, and therefore it fell within the express terms of the ADA's preemption provision. As a result, the substantive provisions of the PBR were subject to preemption.

FEDERAL AVIATION ACT REGULATIONS

The Second Circuit also held that insofar as the PBR was intended to prescribe standards of airline safety, it was also impliedly preempted by the Federal Aviation Act's extensive system of federal regulation in the field of air safety. (In 1994, Congress codified existing aviation legislation in Title 49 of the U.S. Code, and the 1958 Aviation Act was thus repealed.) The Aviation Act was passed by Congress for the purpose of centralizing the power to promulgate rules for the safe and efficient use of the nation's airspace, and this power extended to grounded planes and airport runways. Federal aviation regulations are also not subject to supplementation by state laws. In light of its determination that the PBR was preempted by the ADA, the court felt it unnecessary to address the scope of any Aviation Act preemption.

In conclusion, the court noted that the goals of the PBR were laudable and the circumstances motivating its enactment deplorable, but only the federal government has the authority to enact such a law. As a result, passengers stranded on the tarmac in New York would unfortunately receive no assistance from the state in the form of mandatory snacks and beverages.

21

+ + + + + + + + + + + + + + + + + + +

AGENT OF TRAVEL
A TENSE RELATIONSHIP

+ + + + + + + + + + + + + + + + + + +

TRAVEL ALL OVER THE WORLD V.
SAUDI ARABIAN AIRLINES
73 F.3d 1423 (7th Cir. 1996)

Travel agencies and airlines don't always get along with one another.

Travel All Over the World, along with its president, Ibrahim Elgindy, sued Saudi Arabian Airlines over an unusual dispute that arose when Travel All arranged flights to Saudi Arabia for its clients. In February of 1990, Travel All contracted with the airline to purchase round-trip airline tickets for approximately 180 clients for an annual religious pilgrimage called the Haaj. Travel All's clients planned to rendezvous in New York, and then fly together to Saudi Arabia. Elgindy accompanied the Chicago contingent, but they were delayed by bad weather on their trip into New York, and they missed the flight to Saudi Arabia.

In Elgindy's absence, Saudi Arabia Airlines cancelled the reservations of the Travel All clients who had made it to New York on time, and the airline required these passengers to repurchase their tickets to Saudi Arabia directly from the airline. This, of course, caused Travel All to lose its commissions. The airline apparently told these passengers that Travel All was not a reputable company, that it failed to book reservations to Saudi Arabia for a number of them, and that Elgindy often neglected his clients' problems. The airline allegedly repeated these statements to Travel All's clients after they arrived in Saudi Arabia and required them to rebook their return flights directly through the airline.

Travel All was not amused, and filed suit against Saudi Arabian Airlines for its conduct. The complaint contained seven counts: breach of contract, tortious interference with a business relationship, defamation, slander, fraud, intentional infliction of emotional distress, and additional tortious interference with a business relationship. The airline replied with a motion to dismiss, arguing that such claims were expressly preempted by the Airline Deregulation Act (ADA). After hearing arguments, the district court dismissed the complaint, holding that all seven counts related to the airline's rates, routes, or services, and was therefore preempted by the ADA. Travel All appealed.

BREACH OF CONTRACT

The question before the court was whether the ADA's express preemption provision encompassed the plaintiffs' common-law claims. The appellate court focused on the plain wording of the statute, concluding that the preemption clause did not shelter airlines from lawsuits that sought recovery solely for the airline's breach of its own self-imposed undertakings.

SLANDER AND DEFAMATION

Travel All next argued that the district court erred in concluding that their slander and defamation claims related to airline rates, routes, or services. The appellate court concluded that the allegedly defamatory statements themselves were not "services" provided by the airline within the meaning of the ADA, and were therefore not preempted. Additionally, the court noted that it was difficult to envision how allowing defamation actions against an airline have even the most tenuous economic effect on the rates, routes, or services that the airline offered.

Travel All's suit against Saudi Arabian Airlines could therefore proceed. One can only hope that the next spiritual pilgrimage will allow for more peaceful relations between the airline and its embattled travel agent.

22

+ + + + + + + + + + + + + + + + + + + +

FREQUENT FLIERS
ALL IN THE FINE PRINT

+ + + + + + + + + + + + + + + + + + + +

MONZINGO V. ALASKA AIR GROUP
112 P.3d 655 (Alaska 2005)

This case arose from a class action seeking over a billion dollars filed by Tony Ed Monzingo on behalf of 3.9 million class members. Monzingo was a member of Alaska Airlines' frequent-flyer program, the "Alaska Airlines Mileage Plan," and he had accumulated 542,484 miles, most of which had not yet been redeemed for free travel or other benefits.

Alaska Airlines implemented a number of changes to the Mileage Plan on September 1, 2001. These changes increased the number of miles necessary to redeem peak, first-class, and some international travel awards. Alaska Airlines maintained that this adjustment affected only 16.4 percent of air travel award levels, accounting for only 21 percent of all awards redeemed in 2000. The Mileage Plan's changes also applied retroactively to miles already accrued but not yet redeemed. Mileage Plan members received their first notice that a change would take place on March 30, 2001. Alaska Airlines issued a press release, posted information about the changes on its website, and sent members notification by email in April 2001. Members were also sent a newsletter in late May 2001. In these various publications, Alaska Airlines alerted members that they could redeem their accumulated miles under the old award structure as long as they booked their airline ticket in the subsequent five months for travel prior to August 1, 2002.

It was undisputed that the "Terms and Conditions" of the Mileage Plan specifically reserved the airline's right to make *prospective* changes to the plan. The parties' disagreement centered instead on whether Alaska Airlines reserved the right to make *retroactive* changes to the plan. The "Terms and Conditions" of the Mileage Plan were sent to every new member of the frequent-flyer program, and this document contained the following qualifications:

- Alaska Airlines reserves the right to change the Mileage Plan terms, conditions, partners, mileage credits and/or award levels. This means with prior notice Alaska Airlines may raise award levels or lower mileage levels, add an unlimited number of blackout dates or limit the number of seats available on any or all flights. Also, certain destinations maybe restricted to members. Furthermore, Alaska Airlines reserves the right to terminate the Mileage Plan with advance notice [emphasis added].
- Subject to additions, deletions or revisions at any time . . .
- Accrued mileage and award certificates do not constitute property of the member . . .
- Alaska Airlines and/or Travel Partners are the final authority on qualifying mileages. Alaska Airlines may, at its discretion, elect to authorize additional mileage credit between any two points on its route system . . .

At the end of its "Terms and Conditions" was a section entitled "Important Reminders," in which Alaska Airlines included an additional warning printed in bold type:

All terms and conditions on Mileage Plan awards are subject to change, and the Mileage Plan program is subject to cancellation at any time by Alaska Airlines.

Although there was no plan language that specifically reserved to the airline the right to devalue previously accumulated miles, the Mileage Plan did include a term concerning "previously accumulated mileage." This provision stated:

Alaska Airlines reserves the right to disqualify persons from further participation in the Mileage Plan and to cancel all previously accumulated mileage if in Alaska Airlines['s] sole judgment such persons have violated any of the eligibility, mileage accumulation, award usage or other terms governing the Alaska Airlines Mileage Plan.

PROCEDURAL HISTORY

On February 11, 2002, Monzingo filed a lawsuit alleging breach of contract and breach of the implied covenant of good faith and fair dealing. He sought certification of a class of persons who had accumulated miles through the Mileage Plan prior to September 1, 2001. Monzingo amended his complaint twice: his first amended complaint included additional claims for unconscionability and conversion, and his second amended complaint limited the action to only one claim for breach of contract.

Alaska Airlines moved for summary judgment, which the court granted. Following the superior court's order, Alaska Airlines brought a motion for attorney's fees, which was also granted.

A motion for class certification was filed by Monzingo, but it was rendered moot by the superior court's grant of summary judgment. Monzingo appealed both the order granting summary judgment and the attorney's fee award.

PREEMPTING THE AIRLINE DEREGULATION ACT

The Airline Deregulation Act (ADA) provides that a state "may not enact or enforce a law, regulation, or other provision having the force and effect of law related to a price, route, or service of an air carrier." The U.S. Supreme Court addressed whether state law claims are preempted by the ADA in *American Airlines, Inc. v. Wolens*, which was similar to this case in that it involved a suit against American Airlines for retroactive modification of its frequent flyer program. The *Wolens* opinion held that the ADA preempted the plaintiffs' claims that were based on the Illinois Consumer Fraud and Deceptive Business Practices Act, but did not preempt a state law breach of contract claim. The *Wolens* Court explained that "it did not read the ADA's preemption clause to shelter airlines from suits seeking recovery solely for the airline's alleged breach of its own, self-imposed undertakings."

Although *Wolens* was almost identical on its facts to the instant case, the *Wolens* Court did not address the contract claim on the merits. Alaska Airlines contended that state law principles of contract interpretation should not be applied in this case because they would "enlarge or enhance [Monzingo's] rights based on state laws or policies external to the agreement, as expressly prohibited by *Wolens*."

In the present case, the Alaska Supreme Court acknowledged that *Wolens* did forbid enlargement or enhancement of rights based on state laws or policies, but the court explained that this prohibition did not extend to such contract construction issues as whether an airline has reserved the right to retroactively change rules governing frequent-flyer credits. The *Wolens* Court concluded only that state-law principles should be preempted "to the extent they seek to effectuate the State's public policies, rather than the intent of the parties." Subsequent decisions had interpreted this language to mean that contract actions seeking invalidation of express contract terms, enforcement of equitable remedies, or punitive damages are preempted, because they would "impermissibly enlarge the scope of the proceedings beyond the parties' agreement." But if the parties "seek to enforce a term implied in fact in the agreement based upon the parties' reasonable expectations," no preemption problem is presented.

The U.S. Supreme Court, in the 2014 case of *Northwest, Inc. v. Ginsberg*, upheld this preemption of state law in the frequent flier context:

> The ADA is based on the view that the best interests of airline passengers are most effectively promoted, in the main, by allowing the free market to operate. If an airline acquires a reputation for mistreating the participants in its frequent flyer program (who are generally the airline's most loyal and valuable customers), customers can avoid that program and may be able to enroll in a more favorable rival program.

CONTRACTUAL INTERPRETATION

The court began by examining the plain language of the Mileage Plan to determine whether the terms and conditions of the plan reserved Alaska Airlines' right to make retroactive changes. Next, the court analyzed the reasonable expectations of the parties at the time that Monzingo agreed to the terms of the Mileage Plan. And finally, the court turned to the parties' course of dealing as further evidence of their reasonable expectations of the Mileage Plan.

PLAIN LANGUAGE

The court examined the nature of restrictions that Alaska Airlines informed its members would apply to the Mileage Plan. The inside front cover of the "Terms contained clear language to warn members about possible changes to the plan.

Monzingo contended that these terms gave Alaska Airlines the right to change award levels, as long as the changes did not apply to previously accumulated miles. But, as Alaska Airlines pointed out, it has also informed Mileage Plan members that "accrued mileage and award certificates do not constitute property of the member," and that "Alaska Airlines reserves the right to terminate the Mileage Plan with advance notice." The court concluded that these provisions manifested an intent to clarify that members had no ownership right in the miles they had earned and thus could not expect that the "value" of these miles would not diminish due to changes in the award levels.

REASONABLE EXPECTATIONS OF THE PARTIES

The court explained that, when read as a whole, the contract did not envision a plan in which members redeem awards based on the award structure in place at the time that particular miles were accrued. As Alaska Airlines argued, it would not be reasonable for a customer to expect this because it would create an "administrative nightmare" for the airline and the customer to keep track of the value of miles relative to the status of the plan at the time the flight was taken. Furthermore, there were no provisions in the detailed language of the plan's terms that would lead a member to believe that Alaska Airlines or the member would be required to track award amounts with each modification.

The Mileage Plan was structured to give Alaska Airlines the power to make changes with adequate notice. Monzingo was given notice of the changes in late March 2001. He had 16 months following the date of this announcement to travel on previously accrued miles, and five months after the announcement to book this travel.

COURSE OF DEALING

The court next turned to the course of dealing between Monzingo and Alaska Airlines to determine whether the parties' previous dealings provided additional evidence of their expectations regarding the plan. Alaska Airlines argued that the frequent unilateral changes made by Alaska Airlines to the plan indicated that Monzingo understood the plan was subject to retroactive changes. Alaska Airlines maintained that award levels were increased 12 times since Monzingo joined the plan, and 13 travel awards were discontinued during that time.

At no point prior to this lawsuit did Monzingo call to complain about the changes, although he was admittedly aware of them. The Alaska statute that concerns the course of dealing provides that "express terms of an agreement and an applicable course of dealing or usage of trade shall be construed where reasonable as consistent with each other." The court concluded that Monzingo assented to the numerous changes made by Alaska Airlines, and that his actions provided an additional indication that Alaska Airlines reserved the right to make changes to the value of previously accumulated miles.

Based on the plain language of the plan, the reasonable expectations of the parties, and the parties' course of dealing, the court concluded that Alaska Airlines reserved the right to make retroactive changes to its Mileage Plan with reasonable notice. And Mr. Monzingo had a lot of free flying to do, even with his now devalued miles.

APPENDIX A

+ + + + + + + + + + + + + + + + + + +

KNOW YOUR AIR TRAVEL RIGHTS

+ + + + + + + + + + + + + + + + + + +

In its publication *Fly Rights: A Consumer Guide to Transportation* (found at http://airconsumer.ost.dot.gov/publications/flyrights.htm), the Department of Transportation sets forth some of your rights as an airline passenger, and a number of excerpts on delayed and cancelled flights, overbooking, and lost baggage are included below. The department also publishes *Air Travel Consumer Reports* on flight delays and mishandled baggage, which can be viewed at http://www.dot.gov/airconsumer/air-travel-consumer-reports.

DELAYED AND CANCELLED FLIGHTS

Airlines don't guarantee their schedules, and you should realize this when planning your trip. There are many things that can—and often do—make it impossible for flights to arrive on time. Some of these problems, like bad weather, air traffic delays, and mechanical issues, are hard to predict and often beyond the airlines' control.

If your flight is delayed, try to find out how late it will be. But keep in mind that it is sometimes difficult for airlines to estimate the total duration of a delay during its early stages. In so-called "creeping delays," developments occur that were not anticipated when the carrier made its initial estimate of the length of the delay. Weather that had been forecast to improve can instead deteriorate, or a mechanical problem can turn out to be more complex than initially evaluated. If the problem is with local weather or air traffic control, all flights will probably be late, and there's not much you or the airline can do to speed up your departure. If your flight is experiencing a lengthy delay, you might be better off trying to arrange another flight, as long as you don't have to pay a cancellation penalty or higher fare for changing your reservations. (It is sometimes easier to make such arrangements by phone than at a ticket counter.) If you find a flight on another airline, ask the first airline if it will endorse your ticket to the new carrier; this could save you a fare collection. Remember, however, that there is no rule requiring them to do this.

If your flight is cancelled, most airlines will rebook you on their first flight to your destination on which space is available, at no additional charge. If this involves a significant delay, find out if another carrier has space and ask the first airline to endorse your ticket to the other carrier. Finding extra seats may be difficult, however, especially over holidays and other peak travel times.

Each airline has its own policies about what it will do for delayed passengers waiting at the airport; there are no federal requirements. If you are delayed, ask the airline staff if it will pay for meals or a phone call. Some airlines, often those charging very low fares, do not provide any amenities to stranded passengers. Others may not offer amenities if the delay is caused by bad weather or something else beyond the airline's control. Contrary to popular belief, airlines are not required to compensate passengers whose flights are delayed or cancelled. As discussed in the chapter on overbooking, compensation is required by law only when you are "bumped" from a flight that is oversold. Airlines almost always refuse to pay passengers for financial losses resulting from a delayed flight. If the purpose of your trip is to close a potentially lucrative business deal, give a speech or lecture, attend a family function, or connect to a cruise, you might want to allow a little extra leeway and take an earlier flight. In other words, airline delays and cancellations aren't unusual, and defensive planning is a good idea when time is your most important consideration.

Some flights are delayed on the airport tarmac before taking off or after landing. DOT rules prohibit most U.S. airlines from allowing a domestic flight to remain on the tarmac for more than three hours unless:

> [t]he pilot determines that there is a safety or security reason why the aircraft cannot taxi to the gate and deplane its passengers, or air traffic control advises the pilot that taxiing to the gate (or to another location

operations.

U.S. airlines operating international flights to or from most U.S. airports must each establish and comply with their own limit on the length of tarmac delays on those flights. On both domestic and international flights, U.S. airlines must provide passengers with food and water no later than two hours after the tarmac delay begins. While the aircraft remains on the tarmac, lavatories must remain operable and medical attention must be available if needed.

When booking your flight, remember that a departure early in the day is less likely to be delayed than a later flight, due to "ripple" effects of delays throughout the day. Also, if an early flight does get delayed or cancelled, you have more rerouting options. If you book the last flight of the day and it is cancelled, you could get stuck overnight. You may select a connection (change of planes) over a nonstop or direct flight because of the convenient departure time or lower fare. However, a change of planes always involves the possibility of a misconnection. If you have a choice of connections and the fares and service are equivalent, choose the one with the least-congested connecting airport, so it will be easier to get to your second flight. You may wish to take into consideration the potential for adverse weather if you have a choice of connecting cities. When making your reservation for a connection, always check the amount of time between flights. Ask yourself what will happen if the first flight is delayed; if you don't like the answer, pick another flight or "construct" a connection that allows more time.

OVERBOOKING

Overbooking is not illegal, and most airlines overbook their scheduled flights to a certain extent in order to compensate for "no-shows." Passengers are sometimes left behind or "bumped" as a result. When an oversale occurs, the Department of Transportation (DOT) requires airlines to ask people who aren't in a hurry to give up their seats voluntarily, in exchange for compensation. Those passengers bumped against their will are, with a few exceptions, entitled to compensation.

VOLUNTARY BUMPING

Almost any planeload of airline passengers includes some people with urgent travel needs and others who may be more concerned about the cost of their tickets than about getting to their destination on time. DOT rules require airlines to seek out people who are willing to give up their seats for compensation before bumping anyone involuntarily. Here's how this works: At the check-in or boarding area, airline employees will look for volunteers when it appears that the flight has been oversold. If you're not in a rush to arrive at your next destination, you can give your reservation back to the airline in exchange for compensation and a later flight. But before you do this, you may want to get answers to these important questions:

- When is the next flight on which the airline can confirm your seat? The alternate flight may be just as acceptable to you. On the other hand, if the airline offers to put you on standby on another flight that's full, you could be stranded.
- Will the airline provide other amenities such as free meals, a hotel room, transfers between the hotel and the airport, and a phone card? If not, you might have to spend the money it offers you on food or lodging while you wait for the next flight.

DOT has not mandated the form or amount of compensation that airlines offer to volunteers. DOT does, however, require airlines to advise any volunteer whether he or she might be involuntarily bumped and, if that were to occur, the amount of compensation that would be due. Carriers can negotiate with their passengers for mutually acceptable compensation. Airlines generally offer a free trip or other transportation benefits to prospective volunteers. The airlines give employees guidelines for bargaining with passengers, and they may select those volunteers willing to sell back their reservations for the lowest price. If the airline offers you a free ticket or a transportation voucher in a certain dollar amount, ask about restrictions. How long is the ticket or voucher good for? Is it "blacked out" during holiday periods when you might want to use it? Can it be used for international flights?

INVOLUNTARY BUMPING

DOT requires each airline to give all passengers who are bumped involuntarily a written statement describing their rights and explaining how the carrier decides who gets on an oversold flight and who doesn't. Those travelers who don't get to fly are frequently entitled to denied-boarding compensation in the form of a check or cash. The amount depends on the price of their ticket and the length of the delay:

- If you are bumped involuntarily and the airline arranges substitute transportation that is scheduled to get you to your final destination (including later connections) within one hour of your original scheduled arrival time, there is no compensation.

- If the airline arranges substitute transportation that is scheduled to arrive at your destination between one and two hours after your original arrival time (between one and four hours on international flights), the airline must pay you an amount equal to 200 percent of your one-way fare to your final destination that day, with a $650 maximum.

- If the substitute transportation is scheduled to get you to your destination more than two hours later (four hours internationally), or if the airline does not make any substitute travel arrangements for you, the compensation doubles (400 percent of your one-way fare, $1,300 maximum).

- If your ticket does not show a fare (for example, a frequent-flyer award ticket or a ticket issued by a consolidator), your denied-boarding compensation is based on the lowest cash, check or credit card payment charged for a ticket in the same class of service (e.g., coach, first class) on that flight.

- You always get to keep your original ticket and use it on another flight. If you choose to make your own arrangements, you can request an "involuntary refund" for the ticket for the flight from which you were bumped. The denied-boarding compensation is essentially a payment for your inconvenience.

- If you paid for optional services on your original flight (e.g., seat selection, checked baggage) and you did not receive those services on your substitute flight or were required to pay a second time, the airline that bumped you must refund those payments to you.

Like all rules, however, there are a few conditions and exceptions:

- To be eligible for compensation, you must have a confirmed reservation. A written confirmation issued by the airline or an authorized agent or reservation service qualifies you in this regard even if the airline can't find your reservation in the computer, as long as you didn't cancel your reservation or miss a reconfirmation deadline.

- Each airline has a check-in deadline, which is the amount of time before scheduled departure during which you must present yourself to the airline at the airport. For domestic flights, most carriers require you to be at the departure gate between 10 minutes and 30 minutes before scheduled departure, but some deadlines can be an hour or longer. Check-in deadlines on international flights can be as much as three hours before scheduled departure time. Some airlines may simply require you to be at the ticket/baggage counter by this time; most, however, require that you get all the way to the boarding area. Some may have deadlines at both locations. If you miss the check-in deadline, you may have lost your reservation and your right to compensation if the flight is oversold.

- As noted above, no compensation is due if the airline arranges substitute transportation that is scheduled to arrive at your destination within one hour of your originally scheduled arrival time.

- If the airline must substitute a smaller plane for the one it originally planned to use, the carrier isn't required to pay people who are bumped as a result. In addition, on flights using aircraft with 30 through 60 passenger seats, compensation is not required if you were bumped due to safety-related aircraft weight or balance constraints.

- The rules do not apply to charter flights, or to scheduled flights operated with planes that hold fewer than 30 passengers. They don't apply to international flights inbound to the United States, although some airlines on these routes may follow them voluntarily. Also, if you are flying between two foreign cities—from Paris to Rome, for example—these rules will not apply. The European Commission has a rule on bumpings that occur in an EC country; ask the airline for details, or go to http://ec.europa.eu/transport/passengers/air/air_en.htm.

Airlines set their own "boarding priorities"—the order in which they will bump different categories of passengers in an oversale situation. When a flight is oversold and there are not enough volunteers, some airlines bump passengers with the lowest fares first. Others bump the last passengers to check in. Once you have purchased your ticket, the most effective way to reduce the risk of being bumped is to get to the airport early. For passengers in the same fare class, the last passengers to check in are usually the first to be bumped, even if they have met the check-in deadline. Allow extra time; assume that the roads are backed up, the parking lot is full, and there is a long line at the check-in counter.

Airlines may offer free tickets or dollar-amount vouchers for future flights in place of a check for denied-boarding compensation. However, if you are bumped involuntarily, you have the right to insist on a check if that is your preference. Once you cash the check (or accept the free flight), you will probably lose the ability to pursue more money from the airline later on. However, if being bumped costs you more money than the airline will pay you at the airport, you can try to negotiate a higher settlement with its complaint department. If this doesn't work, you usually have 30 days from the date on the check to decide if you want to accept the amount. You are always free to decline the check (e.g., not cash it) and take the airline to court to try to obtain more compensation. DOT's denied-boarding regulation spells out the airlines' minimum obligation to people they bump involuntarily. Finally, don't be a "no-show." If you are holding confirmed reservations you don't plan to use, notify the airline. If you don't, they will cancel all onward or return reservations on your trip.

BAGGAGE

Between the time you check your luggage in and the time you claim it at your destination, it may have passed through a maze of conveyor belts and baggage carts. Once airborne, baggage may tumble around the cargo compartment if the plane hits rough air. In all fairness to the airlines, however, relatively few bags are damaged or lost. With some common-sense packing and other precautions, your bags will likely be among the ones that arrive safely.

PACKING

You can pack to avoid problems. Certain items should never be put into a piece of luggage that you plan to check into the baggage compartment:

- Small valuables: cash, credit cards, jewelry, an expensive camera.
- Critical items: medicine, keys, passport, tour vouchers, business papers.
- Irreplaceable items: manuscript, heirlooms.
- Fragile items: eyeglasses, glass containers, liquids.

Things like this should be carried on your person or packed in a carry-on bag. Remember, the only way to be sure your valuables are not damaged or lost is to keep them with you. Full flights sometimes run out of room in the cabin for full-size carry-on bags. In those situations the airline must sometimes "gate check" the carry-on baggage of the last passengers to board the flight. This happens near the door to the aircraft. Pack your carry-on bag in a manner so that if it must be gate-checked you can quickly remove the fragile, valuable, and critical items described above. For example, consider packing all such items in a small, soft bag that will fit under the seat in front of you, and make sure that this small bag is easily accessible in your carry-on bag.

Although only a tiny percentage of checked bags are permanently lost, your bag might be delayed for a day or two. Don't put perishables in a checked bag;

they may spoil if it is delayed. It is wise to put items that you will need during the first 24 hours in a carry-on bag (e.g., toiletries, a change of underwear). Check with the airline for its limits on the size, weight, and number of carry-on pieces. As of this writing, on most flights you are allowed to carry on one bag plus one personal item (e.g., purse, briefcase, camera bag, laptop computer bag). If you are using more than one airline, check with all of them. Inquire about your flight; different airplanes can have different limits. Don't assume that the flight will have closet space for every carry-on garment bag; yours may have to be checked. If you plan to go shopping at your destination and bring your purchases aboard as carry-on, keep the limits in mind. If you check these purchases, however, carry the receipts separately; they may be necessary for a claim if the merchandise is lost or damaged. Don't put anything into a carry-on bag that could be considered a weapon (e.g., certain scissors, pocket knives). Check the website of the Transportation Security Administration (TSA) for restrictions on carry-on baggage. (www.tsa.gov, then click "Travelers.")

As with carry-ons, checked baggage is subject to limits. Some airlines permit one or two checked bags at no charge; other carriers charge for even one checked bag. There can also be an extra charge if you exceed the airline's limits on the size, weight, or number of the bags.

On some flights between two foreign cities, your allowance may be lower and may be based primarily on the weight of the checked bags rather than the number of pieces. The same two bags that cost you nothing to check when you started your trip could result in expensive excess-baggage charges under a weight system. Ask the airlines about the limit for every segment of your international trip before you leave home, especially if you have a stopover of a day or two or if you are changing carriers.

The bags you check should be labeled inside and out with your name and phone number. Add the name and phone number of a person to contact at your destination if it's practical to do so. Almost all of the bags that are misplaced by airlines do turn up sooner or later. With proper labeling, the bag and its owner can usually be reunited within a few hours.

Don't overpack a bag. This puts pressure on the latches, making it easier for them to pop open. If you plan to check any glassware, musical instruments or other fragile items, they should be packed in a container specifically designed to survive rough handling, preferably a factory-sealed carton or a padded hard-shell carrying case.

Don't check in at the last minute. Even if you make the flight, your bag may not. If you miss the airline's check-in deadline, the carrier might not assume liability for your bag if it is delayed or lost. If you have a choice, select flights that minimize the potential for baggage disruption. The likelihood of a bag going astray increases from #1 to #4 as follows (i.e., #1 is safest): 1) nonstop flight; 2) direct or 'through' flight (one or more stops, but no change of aircraft); 3) online connection (change of aircraft but not airlines); and 4) interline connection (change of aircraft and airlines).

When you check in, remove straps and hooks from garment bags that you are sending as checked baggage. These can get caught in baggage-processing machinery, causing damage to the bag.

The airline will put baggage destination tags on your luggage and give you the stubs to use as claim checks. Make sure you get a stub for every bag. Don't throw them away until after you get your bags back and you check the contents. Not only will you need them if a claim is necessary, but you may need to show them to security upon leaving the baggage-claim area.

Your bags may only be checked to one of your intermediate stops rather than your destination city if you must clear Customs short of your final destination, or if you are taking a connection involving two airlines that don't have an interline agreement. Be sure all of the tags from previous trips are removed from your bag, since they may cause your bag to go astray.

CLAIMING YOUR BAGS

Many bags look alike. After you pull what you think is your bag off the carousel, check the name tag or the bag tag number. If your bag arrives open, unlocked or visibly damaged, check right away to see if any of the contents are missing or damaged. Report any problems to the airline before leaving the airport; insist on having a report created. Open your suitcase immediately when you get to where you are staying. Any damage to the contents or any pilferage should be immediately reported to the airline by telephone. Make a note of the date and time of the call, and the name and telephone number of the person you spoke with. Follow up as soon as possible with a certified letter to the airline.

DAMAGE

If your suitcase arrives smashed or torn, the airline will usually pay for repairs. If it can't be fixed, they will negotiate a settlement to pay you its depreciated value. The same holds true for belongings packed inside. Airlines may decline to pay for damage caused by the fragile nature of the broken item or inadequate packing, rather than the airline's rough handling. Air carriers might also refuse to compensate you for damaged items inside the bag when there's no evidence of external damage to the suitcase. When you check in, airline personnel may let you know if they think your suitcase or package may not survive the trip intact. Before accepting a questionable item, they may ask you to sign a statement in which you agree to check it at your own risk. But even if you do sign this form, the airline might be liable for damage if it is caused by its own negligence, shown by external injury to the suitcase or package.

DELAYED BAGS

If you and your suitcase don't connect at your destination, don't panic. The airlines have very sophisticated systems that track down the vast majority of misplaced bags and return them to their owners within hours. In many cases they will absorb reasonable expenses you incur while they look for your missing belongings. You and the airline may have different ideas of what's reasonable, however, and the amount it will pay is subject to negotiation.

If your bags don't come off the conveyor belt, report this to airline personnel before you leave the airport. Insist that they create a report and give you a copy, even if they say the bag will be in on the next flight. Get an appropriate phone number for following up (not the Reservations number). Don't assume that the airline will deliver the bag without charge when it is found; ask the airline about this. Most carriers set guidelines for their airport employees that allow them to disburse some money at the airport for emergency purchases. The amount depends on whether or not you're away from home and how long it takes to track down your bags and return them to you. If the airline does not provide you a cash advance, it may still reimburse you later for the purchase of necessities. Discuss with the carrier the types of articles that would be reimbursable, and keep all receipts. If the airline misplaces sporting equipment, it will sometimes pay for the rental of replacements. For replacement clothing or other articles, the carrier might offer to absorb only a portion of the purchase cost, on the basis that you will be able to use the new items in the future. (The airline may agree to a higher reimbursement if you turn the articles over to them.)

When you've checked in fresh foods or any other perishable goods and they are ruined because their delivery is delayed, the airline won't reimburse you. Carriers may be liable if they lose or damage perishable items, but they won't accept responsibility for spoilage caused by a delay in delivery.

Airlines are liable for provable consequential damages up to the amount of their liability limit (see below) in connection with the delay. If you can't resolve the claim with the airline's airport staff, keep a record of the names of the employees with whom you dealt, and hold on to all travel documents and receipts for any money you spent in connection with the mishandling. (It's okay to surrender your baggage claim tags to the airline when you fill out a form at the airport, as long as you get a copy of the form and it notes that you gave up the tags.) Contact the airline's baggage claims office or consumer office when you get home.

LOST LUGGAGE

Once your bag is declared (permanently) lost, you will have to submit a claim. This usually means you have to fill out a second, more detailed form. Check on this; failure to complete the second form when required could delay your claim. Missing the deadline for filing it could invalidate your claim altogether.

The airline will usually refer your claim to a central office, and the negotiations between you and the airline will begin. If your flight was a connection involving two carriers, the final carrier is normally the one responsible for processing your claim even if it appears that the first airline lost the bag. Airlines don't automatically pay the full amount of every claim they receive. First, they will use the information on your form to estimate the value of your lost belongings. Like insurance companies, airlines consider the depreciated value of your possessions, not their original price or the replacement costs. If you're tempted to exaggerate your claim, don't. Airlines may completely deny claims they feel are inflated or fraudulent. They often ask for sales receipts and other documentation to back up claims, especially if a large amount of money is involved. If you don't keep extensive records, you can expect to negotiate with the airline over the value of your goods. Generally, it takes an airline anywhere from four weeks to three months to pay passengers for their lost luggage. When airlines tender a settlement, they may offer you the option of free tickets on future flights in a higher amount than the cash payment. Ask about all restrictions on these tickets, such as "blackout" periods.

LIMITS ON LIABILITY

Airlines assert a limit on their liability for delayed, lost, or damaged checked baggage. When your luggage and its contents are worth more than the liability limit, you may want to purchase "excess valuation," if available, from the airline as you check in. This is not insurance, but it will increase the carrier's potential liability. The airline may refuse to sell excess valuation on some items that are especially valuable or breakable, such as antiques, musical instruments, jewelry, manuscripts, negotiable securities, and cash.

On domestic trips, the airline can invoke a liability ceiling that is regulated by DOT and that is adjusted every two years. On international round-trips that originate in the United States, the liability limit is set by a treaty called the Montreal Convention. This treaty also governs liability on international round-trips that originate in another country that has ratified this Convention, and one-way trips between the U.S. and such a country. The current limits may be listed on your confirmation, or you can find them at http://airconsumer.dot. gov. The international limit applies to domestic segments of an international journey. This is the case even if the domestic and international flights are on separate tickets and you claim and recheck your bag between the two flights.

Keep in mind that the liability limits are maximums. If the depreciated value of your property is worth less than the liability limit, this lower amount is what you will be offered. If the airline's settlement doesn't fully reimburse your loss, check your homeowner's or renter's insurance; it sometimes covers losses away from the residence. Some credit card companies and travel agencies offer optional or even automatic supplemental baggage coverage. Special liability requirements apply to the domestic transportation of assistive devices used by passengers with disabilities. See the publication *New Horizons: Information for the Air Traveler with a Disability* at http://airconsumer.dot.gov/.

COMPLAINING

DOT rules require U.S. airlines to provide information on how to file a complaint with the carrier. This information must appear on their websites, on all e-ticket confirmations, and upon request at any of the airline's ticket counters or gates. When passengers comment on airline service, most airlines do listen. They track and analyze the complaints and compliments they receive and use the information to determine what the public wants and to identify problem areas that need attention. They also try to resolve individual complaints. A DOT rule requires that airlines acknowledge a written complaint within 30 days and send a substantive response within 60 days of receiving the complaint.

Like other businesses, airlines have a lot of discretion in how they respond to problems. While you do have certain rights as a passenger, your demands for compensation will probably be subject to negotiation, and the kind of action you get often depends in large part on the way you go about complaining. Start with the airline. Before you contact DOT for help with an air travel problem, you should give the airline a chance to resolve it. As a rule, airlines have troubleshooters at the airports (they're usually called Customer Service Representatives) who can take care of many problems on the spot. They can often arrange meals and hotel rooms for stranded passengers, write checks for denied-boarding compensation, arrange luggage resolutions, and settle other routine claims or complaints

If you can't resolve the problem at the airport and want to file a complaint, it's best to write or email the airline's consumer office at its corporate headquarters. DOT requires most U.S. airlines to state on their websites how and where complaints can be submitted. There may be a form on the airline's website for this purpose. Take notes at the time the incident occurred and jot down the names of the carrier employees with whom you dealt. Keep all of your travel documents (ticket or confirmation, baggage check stubs, boarding pass, etc.) as well as receipts for any out-of-pocket expenses that were incurred as a result of the mishandling. Here are some helpful tips should you choose to write.

- If you send a letter, type it and, if at all possible, limit it to two pages.
- Include your daytime telephone number (with area code).
- No matter how angry you might be, keep your letter or email businesslike in tone and don't exaggerate what happened. If the complaint sounds very vehement or sarcastic, you might wait a day and then consider revising it.
- Describe what happened, and give dates, cities, and flight numbers or flight times.
- Where possible, include copies, never the originals, of tickets and receipts or other documents that can back up your claim.
- Include the names of any employees who were rude or made things worse, as well as anyone who might have been especially helpful.
- Don't clutter your complaint with a litany of petty gripes that can obscure what you're really angry about.
- Let the airline know if you've suffered any special inconvenience or monetary losses.
- Say just what you expect the carrier to do to make amends. An airline may offer to settle your claim with a check or some other kind of compensation, possibly free transportation. You might want a written apology from a rude employee or reimbursement for some loss you incurred, but the airline needs to know what you want before it can decide what action to take.
- Be reasonable. If your demands are way out of line, you are rude or sarcastic, or you use vulgar language, at best your letter might earn you a polite apology and a place in the airline's crank files.

If you follow these guidelines, the airlines will probably treat your complaint seriously. Your letter will help them to determine what caused your problem, as well as to suggest actions the company can take to keep the same thing from happening to other people.

CONTACTING THE DEPARTMENT OF TRANSPORTATION

Complaints about airline service may be registered with DOT's Aviation Consumer Protection Division (ACPD). You can call, write, or use our web-based complaint form.

You may call the ACPD 24 hours a day at 202-366-2220 (TTY 202-366-0511) to record your complaint.

You may send them a letter at:

Aviation Consumer Protection Division, C-75
U.S. Department of Transportation
1200 New Jersey Ave. S.E.
Washington, D.C. 20590

To send us a complaint, comment or inquiry electronically, please use our web form at http://dot.gov.airconsumer.

FILING A COMPLAINT

If you write, please be sure to include your address and a daytime telephone number, with area code. Complaints from consumers help us spot problem areas and trends in the airline industry. We use our complaint files to document the need for changes in DOT's consumer protection regulations and, where warranted, as the basis for enforcement action (i.e., where a serious breach of the law has occurred). In addition, every month we publish a report with information about the number of complaints we receive about each airline and what problems people are having. You can find this Air Travel Consumer Report on our website, http://dot.gov.airconsumer. That publication also has statistics that the airlines file with us on flight delays, oversales, and mishandled baggage.

If your complaint is about something you feel is a safety hazard, write to the Federal Aviation Administration at:

Federal Aviation Administration
Aviation Safety Hotline, AAI-3
800 Independence Avenue, SW
Washington, D.C. 20591
Or call 1-866-TELL-FAA (1-866-835-5322).

Questions or concerns about aviation security should be directed to the Transportation Security Administration:

Phone (toll-free): 1-866-289-9673
E-mail: TSA-ContactCenter@dhs.gov

Or write to:

Transportation Security Administration
601 South 12th Street
Arlington, VA 20598

U.S. DEPARTMENT OF TRANSPORTATION
Write to:

Aviation Consumer Protection Division, C-75
U.S. Department of Transportation
1200 New Jersey Ave., SE
Washington, D.C. 20590
or visit http://dot.gov.airconsumer

APPENDIX B

+ + + + + + + + + + + + + + + + + + + +

SHOT DOWN

+ + + + + + + + + + + + + + + + + + + +

CHAN V. KOREAN AIR LINES, LTD.
490 U.S. 122 (1989)

JUSTICE SCALIA DELIVERED THE OPINION OF THE COURT

This case presents the question whether international air carriers lose the benefit of the limitation on damages for passenger injury or death provided by the multilateral treaty known as the Warsaw Convention if they fail to provide notice of that limitation in the 10-point type size required by a private accord among carriers, the Montreal Agreement.

I

On September 1, 1983, over the Sea of Japan, a military aircraft of the Soviet Union destroyed a Korean Air Lines, Ltd. (KAL) Boeing 747 en route from Kennedy Airport in New York to Seoul, South Korea. All 269 persons on board the plane perished. Survivors of the victims filed wrongful-death actions against KAL in several Federal District Courts, all of which were transferred for pretrial proceedings to the District Court for the District of Columbia pursuant to 28 U.S.C. § 1407. All parties agree that their rights are governed by the Warsaw Convention, a multilateral treaty governing the international carriage of passengers, baggage, and cargo by air.

The present controversy centers on the per passenger damages limitation for personal injury or death. This was fixed at approximately $8,300 by the Convention, but was raised to $75,000 by the Montreal Agreement, an agreement among carriers executed (and approved by the Civil Aeronautics Board (CAB)) in 1966, and joined by KAL in 1969. In addition to providing for a higher damages limitation, this agreement required carriers to give passengers written notice of the Convention's damage limitations in print size no smaller than 10-point type. The notice of the Convention's liability rules printed on KAL's passenger tickets for the flight in question here appeared in only 8-point type. By motion for partial summary judgment, plaintiffs sought a declaration that this discrepancy deprived KAL of the benefit of the damages limitation.

On July 25, 1985, the District Court for the District of Columbia denied the motion, finding that neither the Warsaw Convention nor the Montreal Agreement prescribes that the sanction for failure to provide the required form of notice is the elimination of the damages limitation. On September 24, 1985, the District Court certified for interlocutory appeal under 28 U.S.C. § 1292(b) the question whether KAL "is entitled to avail itself of the limitation of damages provided by the Warsaw Convention and Montreal Agreement despite its defective tickets." The District of Columbia Circuit allowed the appeal and (following a remand of the record for clarification of the scope of the District Court's order) affirmed, adopting the District Court's opinion in full. We granted certiorari to resolve the conflict among the Courts of Appeals. (In addition to the Second Circuit, the Fifth is in disagreement with the District of Columbia Circuit's resolution here.

II

Petitioners concede that by itself the Montreal Agreement imposes no sanction for failure to comply with its 10-point type requirement. They argue, however, that such a requirement is created by reading the Montreal Agreement in conjunction with the Warsaw Convention. This argument proceeds in two steps. First, petitioners assert that Article 3 of the Warsaw Convention removes the protection of limited liability if a carrier fails to provide adequate notice of the Convention's liability limitation in its passenger tickets. Second, they contend that the Montreal Agreement's 10-point type requirement supplies the standard of adequate notice under Article 3. Because we reject the first point, we need not reach the second.

Article 3 of the Warsaw Convention provides:

> (1) For the transportation of passengers the carriers must deliver a passenger ticket which shall contain the following particulars:
>> (a) The place and date of issue;
>> (b) The place of departure and of destination;
>> (c) The agreed stopping places, provided that the carrier may reserve the right to alter the stopping places in case of necessity, and that if he exercises that right, the alteration shall not have the effect of depriving the transportation of its international character;
>> (d) The name and address of the carrier or carriers;
>> (e) A statement that the transportation is subject to the rules relating to liability established by this convention.
>
> (2) The absence, irregularity, or loss of the passenger ticket shall not affect the existence or the validity of the contract of transportation, which shall none the less be subject to the rules of this convention. Nevertheless, if the carrier accepts a passenger without a passenger ticket having been delivered he shall not be entitled to avail himself of those provisions of this convention which exclude or limit his liability.

Although Article 3(1)*(e)* specifies that a passenger ticket shall contain "[a] statement that the transportation is subject to the rules relating to liability established by this convention," nothing in Article 3 or elsewhere in the Convention imposes a sanction for failure to provide an "adequate" statement. The only sanction in Article 3 appears in the second clause of Article 3(2), which subjects a carrier to unlimited liability if it "accepts a passenger without a passenger ticket having been delivered." Several courts have equated nondelivery of a ticket, for purposes of this provision, with the delivery of a ticket in a form that fails to provide adequate notice of the Warsaw limitation.

We cannot accept this interpretation. All that the second sentence of Article 3(2) requires in order to avoid its sanction is the "deliver[y]" of "a passenger ticket." Expanding this to mean "a passenger ticket in compliance with the requirements of this Convention" is rendered implausible by the first sentence of Article 3(2), which specifies that "[t]he irregularity of the passenger ticket shall not affect the existence or the validity of the contract of transportation, which shall none the less be subject to the rules of this convention." It is clear from this (1) that an "irregularity" does not prevent a document from being a "passenger ticket"; and (2) that an "irregularity" in a passenger ticket does not eliminate the contractual damages limitation provided for by the Convention. "Irregularity" means the "[q]uality or state of not conforming to rule or law," Webster's Second International Dictionary (1950), and in the present context the word must surely refer to the rules established by the Convention, including the notice requirement. Thus, a delivered document does not fail to qualify as a "passenger ticket," and does not cause forfeiture of the damages limitation, merely because it contains a defective notice. When Article 3(2), after making this much clear, continues (in the second sentence) "Nevertheless, if a carrier accepts a passenger without a passenger ticket having been delivered, etc.," it can only be referring to the carrier's failure to deliver any document whatever, or its delivery of a document whose shortcomings are so extensive that it cannot reasonably be described as a "ticket" (for example, a mistakenly delivered blank form, with no data filled in). Quite obviously, the use of 8-point type instead of 10-point type for the liability limitation notice is not a shortcoming of such magnitude; indeed, one might well select that as a polar example of what could not possibly prevent a document from being a ticket.

Besides being incompatible with the language of the Convention, the proposition that, for purposes of Article 3(2), delivering a defective ticket is equivalent to failure to deliver a ticket produces absurd results. It may seem reasonable enough that a carrier "shall not be entitled to avail himself of those provisions of this convention which exclude or limit his liability" when the ticket defect consists precisely of a failure to give the passenger proper notice of those provisions. But there is no textual basis for limiting the "defective-ticket-is-no-ticket" principle to that particular defect. Thus, the liability limitation would also be eliminated if the carrier failed to comply, for example, with the requirement of Article 3(1)*(d)* that the ticket contain the address of the carrier.

The conclusion that defective compliance with the notice provision does not eliminate the liability limitation is confirmed by comparing Article 3(2) with other provisions of the Convention. Article 3 is a part of Chapter II of the Convention, entitled "Transportation Documents." Just as Section I of that Chapter (which includes Article 3) specifies what information must be included in passenger tickets, Sections II and III specify what information must be included in, respectively, baggage checks and air waybills for cargo. All three sections require, in identical terms, "[a] statement that the transportation is subject to the rules relating to liability established by this convention." All three sections also provide, again in identical terms, that if the relevant document (ticket, baggage check, or air waybill) has not been delivered (or, in the case of air waybill, "made out"), the carrier "shall not be entitled to avail himself of the provisions of this convention which exclude or limit his liability." But, *unlike Section I*, Sections II and III also specifically impose the latter sanction for failure to include in the documents certain particulars, including (though not limited to) the notice of liability limitation. Sections II and III thus make doubly clear what the text of Article 3(2) already indicates: that delivery of a defective document is something quite different from failure to deliver a document. And given the parallel structures of these provisions it would be a flouting of the text to imply in Section I a sanction not only withheld there but explicitly granted elsewhere. When such an interpretation is allowed, the art of draftsmanship will have become obsolete.

Petitioners and the United States as *amicus curiae* seek to explain the variance between Section I and Sections II and III (as well as the clear text of Article 3) as a drafting error, and lead us through the labyrinth of the Convention's drafting history in an effort to establish this point. It would be absurd, they urge, for defective notice to eliminate liability limits on baggage and air freight but not on personal injury and death. Perhaps not. It might have been thought, by the representatives from diverse countries who drafted the Convention in 1925 and 1929 (an era when even many States of this country had relatively low limits on wrongful-death recovery) that the $8,300 maximum liability established for personal injury or death was a "fair" recovery in any event, so that even if the defective notice caused the passenger to forgo the purchase of additional insurance, he or his heirs would be treated with rough equity in any event. Quite obviously, however, the limitation of liability for baggage and freight (about $16.50 per kilogram) was not set with an eye to fair value (the very notion of a "fair" average value of goods per kilogram is absurd), but perhaps with an eye to fair level of liability in relation to profit on the carriage—so that the shipper of lost goods misled by the inadequate notice would not be compensated equitably. Another possible explanation for the difference in treatment is that the limitations on liability prescribed for baggage and freight are much more substantial and thus notice of them is much more important. They include not just a virtually nominal monetary limit, but also total exclusion of liability for "an error in piloting, in the handling of the aircraft, or in navigation." Article 20. Or perhaps the difference in treatment can be traced to a belief that people were much more likely, if adequate notice was given, to purchase additional insurance on goods than on their own lives—not only because baggage and freight are lost a lot more frequently than passengers, but also because the Convention itself establishes, in effect, an insurance-purchasing counter at the airport for baggage and freight, providing that if the consignor makes "a special declaration of the value at delivery and has paid a supplementary sum if the case so requires," the carrier will be liable for actual value up to the declared sum.

These estimations of what the drafters might have had in mind are of course speculation, but they suffice to establish that the result the text produces is not necessarily absurd, and hence cannot be dismissed as an obvious drafting error. We must thus be governed by the text—solemnly adopted by the governments of many separate nations—whatever conclusions might be drawn from the intricate drafting history that petitioners and the United States have brought to our attention. The latter may of course be consulted to elucidate a text that is ambiguous. But where the text is clear, as it is here, we have no power to insert an amendment. As Justice Story wrote for the Court more than a century and a half ago:

> [T]o alter, amend, or add to any treaty, by inserting any clause, whether small or great, important or trivial, would be on our part an usurpation of power, and not an exercise of judicial functions. It would be to make, and not to construe a treaty. Neither can this Court supply a *casus omissus* in a treaty, any more than in a law. We are to find out the intention of the parties by just rules of interpretation applied to the subject matter; and having found that, our duty is to follow it as far as it goes, and to stop where that stops—whatever may be the imperfections or difficulties which it leaves behind.

For the reasons given above, we agree with the opinion of the Supreme Court of Canada, that the Warsaw Convention does not eliminate the limitation on damages for passenger injury or death as a sanction for failure to provide adequate notice of that limitation. Accordingly, we affirm the judgment of the District of Columbia Circuit.

So ordered.

JUSTICE BRENNAN, WITH WHOM JUSTICE MARSHALL, JUSTICE BLACKMUN, AND JUSTICE STEVENS JOIN, CONCURRING IN THE JUDGMENT:

If I may paraphrase Justice Harlan: I agree that the interpretation of the Warsaw Convention advanced by petitioners should be rejected, but I consider it entitled to a more respectful burial than has been accorded. Over the last 25 years, petitioners' argument has been accepted, until the present litigation, by virtually every court in this country that has considered it. One such judgment was affirmed here by an equally divided Court. It is a view of the Convention that has consistently been adopted by the Executive Branch, and which is pressed on us in this case by the United States as amicus curiae. It deserves at least to be stated in full, and to be considered without the self-affixed blindfold that prevents the Court from examining anything beyond the treaty language itself.

The Court holds that the sanction of Article 3(2), which consists of the loss of the Convention's limitation on liability under Article 22(1), applies only when no passenger ticket at all is delivered. That is a plausible reading, perhaps even the most plausible reading of the language of the Convention. But it is disingenuous to say that it is the only possible reading. Certainly it is wrong to disregard the wealth of evidence to be found in the Convention's drafting history on the intent of the governments that drafted the document. It is altogether proper that we consider such extrinsic evidence of the treaty makers' intent. The drafters of an international treaty generally are, of course, the instructed representatives of the governments that ultimately ratify the treaty. The record of their negotiations can provide helpful clues to those governments' collective intent, as it took shape during the negotiating process.

There is strong evidence that the drafters of the Warsaw Convention may have meant something other than what the Court thinks that document says. In the first place, the text of the Convention is surely susceptible of an interpretation other than the Court's. Article 3(1) describes as follows what it is the carrier must deliver: "[A] passenger ticket which shall contain the following particulars . . . ." I think it not at all unreasonable to read the term "passenger ticket," when used subsequently in Article 3(2), as shorthand for this longer phrase. The first sentence of Article 3(2), moreover, *quite clearly* does not have the meaning the Court ascribes to it. That sentence provides that the "absence, irregularity, or loss" of a ticket shall not affect the validity of the contract, "which shall none the less be subject to the rules of this convention." Those rules include the one laid down in the very next sentence, *i. e.*, the provision for loss of the liability limitation. Thus, there exists a contract even if the ticket is absent or "irregular," and that contract is still governed by *all* of the provisions of the Convention, one of which denies the carrier the benefit of the liability limit under certain conditions. The intent of Article 3(2), as a whole, is surely to hold the carrier to the obligations, but to deny it the benefits, of the Convention, if it fails to comply with certain requirements.

Thus, the language of Article 3 does not, to say the least, exclude the interpretation that failure to provide the required notice results in loss of the limitation on liability. On the other hand, the difference between the language of Article 3 and that of Articles 4 and 9 casts some doubt on that reading.

Evidence from the drafting history of the Convention is therefore helpful in understanding what the contracting governments intended.

The Convention was drafted between the first and second international conferences on private aviation law, held, respectively, in Paris in 1925 and Warsaw in 1929. The drafting work was done by a committee of experts, CITEJA, and particularly by the committee's Second Commission, during a series of meetings in 1927 and 1928. See generally M. Smirnoff, Le Comite International Technique d'Experts Juridiques Aeriens (1936). The text CITEJA presented at the Second International Conference on Private Aviation Law in Warsaw in 1929 was amended in a number of respects before its adoption and submission to the several governments for ratification. Without tracing the evolution of the draft convention in detail, several important themes can be discerned from CITEJA's drafts and minutes.

First, it is abundantly clear that throughout the entire drafting process the delegates intended to apply the same regime of sanctions for failure to comply with the provisions concerning passenger tickets, baggage checks, and air waybills. The initial object of CITEJA's work was the preparation of a convention on the air waybill for the transport of freight. In this phase, its draft contained the requirement that the waybill include various "particulars" (Article 7), as well as a statement that the transportation was subject to the Convention's rules relating to liability (Article 8). The sanction for failure to comply was clear: "If an air waybill containing all the particulars set out in Article 7(a) through (g) and by Article 8 has not been made out for international transportation, the carrier shall still be subject to the rules of the International Convention on liability, but the carrier shall not be entitled to avail himself of those provisions of this Convention that exclude his own liability, release him from responsibility for the errors of his agents, or limit his liability."

Subsequently, CITEJA determined to merge the air waybill convention with proposed modifications to an international liability convention adopted in 1925. At the third session of CITEJA in May 1928, the Second Commission presented a draft convention which, in its Article 3, contained provisions similar to those foreseen for the air waybill in the previous draft. Thus, the passenger ticket was to include four listed particulars, as well as "a statement that the transportation is subject to the rules relating to liability established by this Convention." The same Article, as amended during the session, provided: "If, for international transportation, the carrier accepts a passenger without a passenger ticket having been made out, or if the ticket does not contain the above-mentioned particulars, the contract is still subject to the rules of this Convention, but the carrier shall not be entitled to avail himself of those provisions of this convention which totally or partially exclude his direct liability or liability derived from the negligence of his agents." Similar provisions were adopted in regard to the baggage check. The report submitted by Henry de Vos, Reporter of the Second Committee, to the full CITEJA, made crystal clear the parallelism of approach adopted for the three types of transportation documents: "[T]he sanction for transporting passengers without regular tickets is the same as that for the transportation of baggage and of goods." Similarly, the report Monsieur de Vos prepared on behalf of CITEJA to accompany its final draft of the Convention contained the following observation: "[T]he sanction provided . . . for carriage of passengers without a ticket *or with a ticket not conforming to the Convention* is identical to that provided . . . for carriage of baggage and goods."

A second observation that can be drawn from the drafting history relates to the purpose of the sanctions clause. This was simply the means chosen by the drafters to compel the air carriers to include on the transportation documents certain "particulars" thought necessary. During the initial stages the drafters had considered requiring the adhering states to impose criminal or civil penalties for failure to comply with the Convention's specifications, but they ultimately accepted a British suggestion that loss of the Convention's benefits should be used as the means of compelling compliance. Thus, the sanction was applied to the failure to include on the transportation documents all of the particulars thought to be essential, but not to certain others whose inclusion was merely recommended. The term "obligatory" was frequently used to refer to the former group. The obligatory particulars were, generally speaking, those relating to the international character of the transportation. These included "[t]he name and address of the carrier." One might today deem that particular unnecessary to demonstrate the international character of the transportation, but that was apparently not the judgment of the drafters, who debated precisely this sort of question, and who saw the severe penalty as being the only practicable means of compelling the carriers to include on the travel documents the particulars the drafters considered essential. (The carrier's address might also have been thought necessary to establish the carrier's domicile for jurisdictional purposes under Article 28.) Thus, what the Court considers an "absurd resul[t]" was one precisely intended (at least until the draft reached the Conference floor) by the authors of the Warsaw Convention.

Several conclusions can be drawn from the final draft CITEJA submitted to the Warsaw Conference. First, it is absolutely clear that under this draft the carrier was to lose the benefit of the liability limitation if it delivered a passenger ticket that did not contain the listed particulars. What is somewhat less clear is whether the clause stipulating that the transportation was subject to the liability provisions of the Warsaw Convention was among those "particulars." Article 3 referred to "the particulars indicated here above"; and while the clause in question was mentioned just above, it was not listed under a letter of the alphabet like the others, but was in a separate paragraph.

The parallel provision of Article 4, on the baggage check, was even more ambiguous on this point: while there, too, the liability clause was referred to in a separate paragraph, following particulars lettered (a) through (f), the penalty provision referenced only the failure to issue a ticket that included particulars (a) through (d). The provisions on the air waybill, on the other hand, specified clearly that failure to include the liability statement would result in loss of the liability limit.

At Warsaw, the Japanese delegation, recognizing the just-mentioned ambiguity, proposed an amendment to Articles 3 and 4, which resulted in the reordering of the liability clause as a lettered "particular." The purpose of the change was to make clear that the liability clause was to be treated as obligatory, *i.e.*, that its omission would result in loss of the limit on liability. This amendment was apparently regarded merely as a technical question of wording, and it engendered no floor discussion. Had only this amendment been adopted, it would have been clear beyond doubt that failure to include the required statement on the passenger ticket would result in loss of the liability limit. But a second relevant amendment was also adopted, and it produced a much more ambiguous document.

Throughout CITEJA's work on the draft Convention, the Greek delegation had repeatedly objected to the sanctions clause as too harsh. Its effort at the May 1928 CITEJA meeting to weaken the sanction, by specifying that it should apply only when prejudice was caused by the omission of a particular, was rejected. But at Warsaw, for reasons which do not emerge from the record, a similar Greek amendment met with more success. The preparatory committee accepted it to the extent of deleting from Article 3(2) the words, "or if the ticket does not contain the particulars indicated above." The parallel provision in Article 4 was treated somewhat differently. A change was made in which particulars were deemed obligatory, but three—including the liability statement, which became particular *(h)*—remained so; thus, the phrase used in the sanctions clause was "or if the baggage check does not contain the particulars set out at *(d)*, *(f)*, and *(h)* above." Articles 8 and 9, concerning the air waybill, were rewritten in a similar fashion.

It is not clear what the reason is for the difference between the final structure of Article 3, on one hand, and Articles 4 and 9, on the other. The Solicitor

General views it essentially as a drafting error, resulting from a failure to coordinate the Japanese and Greek amendments. It is, to be sure, possible that the drafters intended to create a different regime for the passenger ticket than for the baggage check and the air waybill. The latter reading draws some support from the Reporter's explanation of the changes made in Article 4 concerning the baggage check: "The last paragraph was not modified like Article 3; that is to say that we have retained the same sanctions in the case of errors in the particulars . . . ." But it is puzzling that such a departure from the fundamental principle of applying the same scheme of sanctions to the passenger ticket, the baggage check, and the waybill would have been made without explanation or acknowledgment. As late as the opening substantive session of the Warsaw Conference itself the CITEJA Reporter, Monsieur de Vos, made clear, as he had at the foregoing CITEJA sessions, the principle of parallel treatment of these three documents. Only four days later Monsieur de Vos himself presented to the convention the preparatory committee's revision of Article 3; and it is difficult to imagine that, had such a fundamental change on this point been intended, he would not have said so explicitly.

An examination of the Greek proposal that led to the change, as well as what Monsieur de Vos said in presenting it, strengthens the impression that no different treatment of the passenger ticket was intended. The Greek proposal referred to the possibility that the carrier might lose its liability limitation because "by simple negligence the carrier has omitted to mention in the passenger ticket the place of issuance, or the point of departure, or his name and address; or even that he keep his former address in the ticket, or finally he does not point out an intermediate stop." The Reporter, in presenting the revision of Article 3 to the plenary session, characterized the Greek concern as follows: "[T]he sanction is too severe when it's a question of a simple omission, of the negligence of an employee of the carrier . . . ." The focus thus appears to have been on clerical errors in filling in the ticket forms. An intent to remove such errors from the list of those that trigger the sanction—as was done also in Article 4 (but not in Article 8)—would not be incompatible with the intent to retain the sanction for failure to include the liability statement, which would hardly result from the same kind of ticket-counter error.

While the record that has been preserved makes it impossible to say with certainty what the treaty makers at Warsaw intended, the explanation that they contemplated only the removal of the four initial particulars from the scope of the sanctions clause finds considerable support in the available evidence. Since at the time the Greek amendment was discussed the liability statement constituted a separate paragraph, rather than being listed as letter *(e)* as it later was, it is conceivable that the preparatory committee removed the words "or if the ticket does not contain the particulars indicated above," without intending to make the liability statement any less obligatory here than in Articles 4 and 9.

The Court offers several hypotheses as to why the drafters of the Convention might have determined to treat the notice requirement differently for the passenger ticket and the baggage check. Such explanations are, however, difficult to square with the actual history of the Convention's drafting. The final text clearly imposes sanctions for omission of the notice in Article 4, whereas Article 3 is ambiguous on this point; but this was not the case in the draft CITEJA presented to the conference. There, if anything, the sanction applied more clearly to the failure to give notice under Article 3 than under Article 4. If there was any reason, therefore, for according the notice requirement less weight in Article 3 than in Article 4, it must have emerged at the Warsaw Conference itself. But there is no trace of such a purpose in the Warsaw minutes, as there surely would have been had a decision been made to reverse the relative treatment of the Article 3 and 4 sanctions provisions in the previous draft. It seems much more likely, therefore, that the difference between Articles 3 and 4 on this point was an unintended consequence of other changes that were made at the conference.

Even if we agree, however, that Article 3 of the Warsaw Convention removes the liability limit for failure to provide notice that the transportation is governed by the Convention's liability provisions, that does not end the matter.

Respondent Korean Air Lines undeniably did give petitioners such notice. Petitioners' argument goes beyond this, however, and requires us to determine whether there exists a requirement that the notice given be "adequate," and, if so, whether the notice provided in this case met that standard.

Courts in this country have generally read an "adequate notice" requirement into the Warsaw Convention. Thus, notice has been held to be inadequate when it was provided under conditions that did not permit the passenger to act on it (by, for example, purchasing additional insurance). Closer to the present situation is the much-noted case of *Lisi v. Alitalia-Linee Aeree Italiane, S.p.A.* There the court characterized the Warsaw Convention notice given by the carrier in 4-point type as "camouflaged in Lilliputian print in a thicket of 'Conditions of Contract'" and as "virtually invisible." The court therefore held that the ticket had not been "'delivered to the passenger in such a manner as to afford him a reasonable opportunity to take self-protective measures . . . .'" More recently two appellate courts, relying on the Montreal Agreement, have held notice in 8.5-point and 9-point type to be inadequate.

If notice is indeed required, it must surely meet some minimal standard of "adequacy." All would agree, no doubt, that notice that literally could be read

only with a magnifying glass would be no notice at all. *Lisi*, of course, presents
a more difficult case. In my view it may well have been correctly decided. But
there is a substantial difference between 4-point and 8-point type, particularly
where, as here, the notice took the form of the "advice" prescribed by the Montreal Agreement and occupied a separate page in the ticket book. It cannot be
said that the notice given here was "camouflaged in Lilliputian print in a thicket
of [other conditions]."

The *Warsaw* and *New Orleans* courts did not, of course, find that to be the
case where notice was given in 8.5- and 9-point type. Rather, those courts
adopted a bright-line rule based on the provision of the Montreal Agreement
that requires notice printed in 10-point type. Petitioners here similarly contend that the Montreal Agreement established a bright line which should be
taken to define what notice is adequate. I cannot accept this argument. The
Montreal Agreement is a private agreement among airline companies, which
cannot and does not purport to amend the Warsaw Convention. To be sure, the
Agreement was concluded under pressure from the United States Government,
which would otherwise have withdrawn from the Warsaw Convention. And
most air carriers operating in the United States are required by Federal Aviation
Administration (FAA) Regulations to become parties to the agreement. But
neither the Montreal Agreement nor the federal regulations purport to sanction failure to provide notice according to the Agreement's specifications with
loss of the Warsaw Convention's limits on liability. The sanction, rather, can
be only whatever penalty is available to the FAA against foreign airlines that
fail to abide by the applicable regulations, presumably including suspension or
revocation of the airline's permit to operate in the United States.

Nor does the Solicitor General contend in this case that the Montreal
Agreement provides for loss of the liability limit in the event of failure to give
the specified notice in 10-point type. His argument is, rather, that the Montreal Agreement and the FAA regulation codified at 14 C.F.R. § 221.175(a)
(1988) set a clear and reasonable standard which the courts should adopt as a
measure of "adequate notice." Brief for United States as *Amicus Curiae* 24-27.
Here, however, the notice given was surely "adequate" under any conventional
interpretation of that term. That being so, I cannot agree that we have any
license to require that the notice meet some higher standard, merely for the
sake of a bright line.

This case is, in my view, far more complex and difficult than the Court would
have it. I am prepared to accept petitioners' position that the Warsaw Convention does sanction failure to provide notice of its applicability with loss of its
limit on liability. Having come that far, I think one must agree as well that

notice that is not minimally legible, at the least, is no notice at all. But I cannot make the leap from there to the view that KAL's 8-point notice was inadequate, as a matter of interpretation of the Warsaw Convention, simply because of the carrier's obligation under a related agreement to provide 10-point notice. I therefore concur in the Court's judgment that respondent has not lost the benefit of the Convention's limit on liability because of the size of the type used in its notice.

[NOTE: Case citations and footnotes have been omitted.]

APPENDIX C

+ +

ON STANDBY

+ +

CONTINENTAL AIR LINES, INC. V. DOLE
784 F.2d 1245 (5th Cir. 1986)

W. EUGENE DAVIS, CIRCUIT JUDGE:

Continental appeals, as too low, an award of the Civil Aeronautics Board (CAB), for providing compulsory standby air service from Honolulu, Hawaii, to Pago Pago, American Samoa between January 31, 1982, and May 13, 1982. Continental argues that the method of arriving at the award denied it procedural due process, that the order was not supported by substantial evidence and that the denial of compensation for certain time periods is contrary to the Federal Aviation Act and the Fifth Amendment of the United States Constitution. We find no error and affirm.

I. BACKGROUND

The Federal Aviation Act allows a carrier providing essential air service to a community to terminate that service after giving ninety days advance notice. 49 U.S.C. § 1389(a)(3). If no other carrier can replace that service, the CAB may require the original carrier to maintain service after the notice period ends and until a replacement carrier is found. When the carrier is required to maintain service beyond the ninety-day notice period, the Board must compensate the carrier for losses incurred in following the Board's order.

Continental provided air service between Pago Pago and Honolulu from 1977 until December 1981. On December 28, 1981, Continental notified the CAB that it intended to terminate its service along the Pago Pago route in ninety days. Ordinarily, an air carrier must continue essential service until the expiration of the ninety-day notice period but because another carrier agreed to serve Pago Pago beginning January 31, 1982, the CAB allowed Continental to end its service on that date. Because the Board was concerned with the reliability of the replacement carrier, the CAB required Continental to remain ready on twenty-four hours notice to resume Pago Pago service should the replacement carrier's service falter. Continental provided this backup service until May 13, 1982, when the CAB permitted it to withdraw from this reserve role.

Continental petitioned the Board for compensation from February 1, 1982, the date it began its backup service until its backup service terminated on May 13, 1982. Continental claims that maintenance of its state of readiness to backup the Pago Pago service cost $1,941,595. To support this figure, Continental filed numerous exhibits and affidavits with the Board. The Board, based on the evidence submitted by Continental and an audit conducted by the Board's staff, awarded Continental $21,394. Continental submitted additional evidence and petitioned for an increase in what it considered a grossly inadequate award. The Board considered Continental's petition and supporting documentary evidence and tentatively increased the award to $39,208 and issued an order to show cause why that award should not become final. Continental again complained that the award was too low and submitted more evidence to support its position. Continental also requested an informal conference with the Board and a formal hearing to assist the Board in resolving the dispute. The Board denied Continental's request for a hearing but after two informal conferences in which Continental's representatives met with the Board's staff, the Board increased the award to $237,390. Continental's appeal brings the dispute over the amount of the award to this court.

Continental asserts that the facts found by the Board in this case fit neatly within the model for adjudicative facts which answer the questions of who did what, where, when, how, why, and with what motive or intent. Continental contends that when an adjudicative, as opposed to a legislative fact finding function is performed, an administrative agency must provide a trial-type hearing on the record. The Board, on the other hand, argues that the award of compensation to Continental was a policy decision involving cost allocation closely tied to rate-making and that such determinations are legislative in nature. The Board argues that in cases such as this involving largely policy decisions, formal trial-type hearings are not as important. The Board also contends that in cases of this type greater deference should be given to the agency's expertise.

These two types of fact finding—adjudicative and legislative—often overlap and are frequently difficult to distinguish. Assuming, without deciding, that the determination of the award in this case was an adjudicative rather than a legislative process, we conclude that under the peculiar circumstances of this case, Continental received all the process that was due it.

"Due process is an elusive concept. Its exact boundaries are undefinable, and its content varies according to specific factual contexts." To determine what process was due Continental we start with a consideration of the three-part balancing test adopted by the Supreme Court in *Mathews v. Eldridge*:

First, the private interest that will be affected by the official action; second, the risk of an erroneous deprivation of such interest through the procedures used, and the probable value, if any, of additional or substitute procedural safeguards; and finally, the Government's interest, including the function involved and the fiscal and administrative burdens that the additional or substitute procedural requirement would entail.

Continental's private interest in this case is an economic one. It is seeking a substantial award for providing backup air service for three and one-half months. There is no contention that the award of less than the amount claimed will significantly affect its ability to continue in business or continue as a viable corporate entity.

The third *Eldridge* factor calls for a consideration of the additional fiscal and administrative burdens placed on the Board if it is required to provide formal hearings in all applications made to it for compensation. The record does not contain the facts necessary for a reasoned analysis of this factor. We do not know the number of claims for compensation that would potentially require a hearing or any peculiar problems the Board would face if it were required to conduct a formal hearing in every case. We assume that such a requirement would place minimal burdens on the Board.

The crucial element in this balancing test when applied to this case is the second factor which requires us to balance the risk of: "An erroneous deprivation of [the private] interest through the procedures used" against the "probable value, if any, of additional or substitute procedural safeguards."

As we stated in *Buttrey* "[a]ny inquiry under the second *Eldridge* heading must necessarily be very fact-specific. . . . [A] slight modification of the facts, suddenly smack[s] . . . of administrative tyranny."

Continental's most serious complaint is that it should have been permitted to cross-examine the staff members who prepared the audit relied upon by the Board in arriving at an award for ownership expenses. This contention requires an examination of the facts that were in dispute before the Board on this issue. Broadly stated, the critical question was whether an entire airplane was devoted to the backup service for the Pago Pago run. Continental asserted that the audit figures and statistics revealed a significantly reduced utilization rate for the DC-10's in its Los Angeles fleet during the time it performed backup service. Continental attributes this reduced utilization rate to the fact that it had an extra airplane in its fleet available to provide the Pago Pago backup service. The Board agreed that the utilization of Continental's aircraft was somewhat lower during the February to May 1982 period than it had been in the summer and fall, but that "although such an aircraft was available for backup duties, it was used to back up Continental's system and not just held out for a potential Pago Pago obligation."

The Board, based on the opinions and judgment of its staff, concluded that the reduced utilization of the aircraft in Continental's Los Angeles fleet was not inordinately low for the winter and spring months when transcontinental air traffic is historically at its low point. The conclusion and reasoning of the staff that led it to this conclusion was fully set forth in the staff report which was issued on June 3, 1982 and to which Continental replied on July 13, 1982. Continental was given the unrestricted right to refute the staff report through the written reports of its experts and briefs of counsel. Also, Continental's counsel met face-to-face with the staff members and had every opportunity to persuade the staff members to accept their point of view or to correct any misunderstandings. It is doubtful that cross-examination of these staff auditors would have served any purpose. If skilled counsel in face-to-face meetings and multiple written submissions was unable to persuade the staff of its error and convince them to accept Continental's point of view, there is little reason to believe that cross-examination would have accomplished any purpose. The value of cross-examination "is often negligible where the dispute turns on matters of expert judgment rather than veracity." We conclude therefore that there is little likelihood that cross-examination of the staff auditors would have been helpful to the Board in reaching an accurate decision.

In summary, we conclude that Continental's property interest is important but not of critical importance. The record is sparse on the additional burdens that will be placed on the agency if it is required to conduct trial-type procedures in every claim for compensation; it is reasonable to infer that the additional burdens would be minimal. Finally and most important, there is little chance that imposition of trial-type procedures with oral cross-examination of witnesses in this case would reduce the chance of error. It follows that Continental's contention that it was denied procedural due process because its demand for a formal hearing and on the record cross-examination of the Board's staff must be rejected. We also reject Continental's bare bones arguments that it was denied due process because no record was made of the informal hearings and that the Board was not impartial. The documents filed by Continental and the Board staff provide an adequate record for review. We find no record support for Continental's argument that the Board was not an impartial decision maker. The fact that the Board relied on its own staff for assistance in evaluating Continental's claim is insufficient to support Continental's argument on this point. We conclude that Continental was given all the process it was due under the Constitution.

III. SUPPORT FOR THE BOARD'S FINDINGS

Continental next argues that the final order of the CAB is not supported by substantial evidence. This contention requires a consideration of the record evidence.

In order to comply with the backup obligation, Continental contends that it expended sums in three areas: flight attendant costs, pilot salaries, and aircraft ownership expenses. We now turn to a consideration of the evidence and Continental's contentions in each of these categories.

A. RESERVE FLIGHT ATTENDANT COSTS.

Continental contends that it was required to keep thirty-seven flight attendants on reserve in Los Angeles at a cost of $148,733 to provide the backup service to Pago Pago. The Board awarded $98,991 to Continental for this item based on its conclusion that only twenty-five attendants were actually needed to fly the Pago Pago route. The Board concluded that the other twelve attendants were reserves and not actually required to perform the essential service. Continental contends that it needed twelve reserve flight attendants to backup the twenty-five attendants needed for a flight. The Board did not abuse its discretion in awarding compensation for only twenty-five flight attendants and in declining to allow compensation for reserves to back up reserves.

B. Reserve pilot costs.

Continental contends that it is entitled to $184,645 instead of the $122,226 awarded by the Board for maintaining eleven reserve pilots to satisfy the backup obligation. The Board found that from March 29, 1982, through April 30, 1982, an average of eleven pilots was maintained on standby status in Honolulu for the Pago Pago flight, but that from May 1 to May 13, 1982, an average of only 2.5 pilots was on standby in Honolulu for this purpose. The remaining 8.5 pilots for whom compensation was claimed were stationed in Los Angeles. The Board concluded that the reserve pilots stationed in Los Angeles were not used to back up the Pago Pago flight. The Board therefore awarded Continental $122,226 out of the $184,645 it claimed for this item. The Board did not abuse its discretion in reaching this conclusion.

C. Aircraft ownership expenses.

Continental finally argues that the $7,168 the Board awarded for aircraft ownership expenses is only a fraction of the $410,899 it cost Continental to own a single airplane during the backup period to comply with the backup obligation. Continental concedes that it did not keep a single identifiable aircraft ready to make the Pago Pago run. Continental contends, however, that it arranged to have extra aircraft in Los Angeles to fly the Pago Pago route if necessary. The staff audit, that was accepted by the Board, revealed that, although an aircraft was always available in Los Angeles to fly the Pago Pago run on twenty-four hours notice, that same airplane was also available to backup Continental's entire Los Angeles system. The staff found that the backup DC-10 aircraft in Los Angeles was in fact used from time-to-time to substitute for other DC-10 aircraft, for B-727 aircraft and for aircraft on military charters. Based primarily on these opinions of its staff, the Board awarded Continental a percentage of the total cost of backing up its entire Los Angeles system. This percentage was based on the ratio of air miles in the Honolulu to Pago Pago run to the air miles customarily flown by the entire Los Angeles fleet. Continental contends that if it had not been required to back up the Pago Pago flight, it would have used fewer reserve aircraft in Los Angeles and could have increased the utilization rate of its fleet. The Board did not abuse its discretion in rejecting this argument. The Board concluded that the low DC-10 utilization during the period

the backup obligation was in effect did not result from the backup obligation
but was caused by the seasonal nature of air traffic which peaks in the summer
months and declines in the winter and spring. This conclusion was buttressed
by Continental's utilization rate for DC-10 aircraft in the previous year, 1981.

Evaluating the significance of the lower utilization rate of Continental's
DC-10 aircraft from December-May 1982 was largely a judgment call. The
expertise of the Board was particularly helpful in making this evaluation and
we are unable to say the Board abused its discretion in the method it chose to
compute the award or in the conclusion it reached.

IV. ADDITIONAL CLAIMS FOR COMPENSATION

Continental argues that in addition to being compensated from the end of the
ninety-day notice period until the termination of the backup requirement it is
also entitled to compensation for fulfilling the backup requirement *during* the
ninety day notice period. (January 31-March 28, 1982). It also contends that it
is entitled to compensation for the cost it incurred in reintegrating the backup
aircraft into its system after the backup requirement was terminated. Continental contends that it is entitled to compensation during these time periods
under the Federal Aviation Act (FAA) or alternatively under the taking clause
of the fifth amendment.

The Board denied Continental's claim for compensation during the ninety-
day notice period under the authority of section 419(a)(7)(B) of the FAA.
This section provides that when a previously uncompensated carrier has been
"providing air transportation to any eligible point without compensation . . .
the Board shall compensate such air carrier for any losses that the air carrier
incurs . . . *after the last day of such 90 day period.* . . ." Continental contends that it
is entitled to compensation during this period under the provisions of section
419(a)(5) of the FAA, which states that: "[t]he Board shall make payments of
compensation under this subsection at times and in a manner determined by
the Board to be appropriate. . . ." In view of the clear express language of section
419(a)(7)(B), we agree with the Board that section 419(a)(5) is designed to give
the Board discretion over the *timing* of the payment of compensation and does
not give the Board discretion in determining the *period* for which compensation
is due. Thus, we agree with the Board that the FAA does not authorize payment
to Continental for costs incurred during the ninety-day notice period.

Continental also contends that the authorization for payment "for any
losses" after the ninety-day notice period under section 419(a)(7)(B) of the
Act includes the cost of reintegrating their aircraft back into their system. The
Board did not abuse its discretion in denying recovery of these costs on grounds

that they would have been incurred by the carrier after it terminated service along the Pago Pago route regardless of whether the backup requirement had been imposed.

Finally, Continental argues that the denial of compensation during the ninety-day notice period and during the reintegration period is an unconstitutional taking without just compensation under the fifth amendment. Continental relies on *Brooks-Scanlon Co. v. Railroad Commission*, which held that the state could not force Brooks-Scanlon Company, an unprofitable railroad, to stay in business and continue operation without compensation. Today's case is readily distinguishable from *Brooks-Scanlon*. Unlike the railroad, Continental did not wish to terminate business entirely; Continental terminated service on one route and was required to provide backup service only on that single route. Justice Holmes, speaking for the Court in *Brooks-Scanlon*, recognized that: "[I] f a railroad continues to exercise the power conferred upon it by a charter from the state, the state may require it to fulfill an obligation imposed by the charter, even though fulfillment in that particular may cause a loss."

[A second distinction is that in *Brooks-Scanlon* the plaintiff was forced to continue its unprofitable railroad operations indefinitely and presumably until it became insolvent, whereas Continental was only required to fulfill the backup obligation without compensation for a limited period. That limited service did not result in dire financial hardship to Continental. The Third Circuit in *Lehigh and New England Railway Co. v. ICC*, distinguished *Brooks-Scanlon* in a similar fashion and held that a railroad carrier could be ordered to operate without compensation *temporarily* over the lines of another carrier unable or unwilling to provide essential rail service.

It is not unreasonable to require an airline to give ninety days notice of its intention to terminate service along a particular route. Continental could have continued flying the route during the notice period and derived revenues from that operation but chose not to do so. Ninety days notice is a reasonable governmental regulation that does not rise to the level of a "taking." "Government hardly could go on if, to some extent, values incident to property could not be diminished without paying for every such change in the general law." We conclude that the denial of compensation during the ninety-day notice period and the reintegration period does not constitute a taking under the fifth amendment.

The final order of the CAB is AFFIRMED.

[NOTE: Case citations and footnotes have been omitted.]

APPENDIX D

+ +

RECONFIRMATION

+ +

LATHIGRA V. BRITISH AIRWAYS PLC
41 F.3d 535 (9th Cir. 1994)

MELVIN T. BRUNETTI, CIRCUIT JUDGE:

Appellants were British Airways passengers returning from Seattle to Madagascar, with a connecting flight on Air Mauritius from Nairobi to Antananarivo. Days before the flight in September 1989, their agent (i.e., the relative whom they had been visiting in Seattle) called British Airways ("BA") to reconfirm the booking. BA, which had itself issued the tickets, reconfirmed appellants' reservations, but neglected to inform them that the Air Mauritius flight had been discontinued. Appellants were stranded in Nairobi for five days and thereby incurred various damages.

In August 1992, they brought a negligence action in Washington state court. BA removed, arguing that the case presented a federal question because the conduct at issue came within the scope of the Warsaw Convention ("the

Convention"), and then moved for summary judgment on the ground that the suit was time-barred. The district court granted BA's motion for summary judgment of dismissal and denied appellants' cross-motion to remand to state court. We reverse, holding that the Convention did not govern BA's conduct here.

DISCUSSION

We review *de novo* the district court's grant of summary judgment. Removal of a case from state to federal court is an exercise of federal subject matter jurisdiction which we also review *de novo*.

BA removed the case to the Western District of Washington on the ground that its actions fell under the Convention, a treaty to which the United States is a party. The Convention provides only a two-year statute of limitations for damages actions. If the Convention governs this action, federal question jurisdiction is proper but the suit is then time-barred. By contrast, Washington's statute of limitations for negligence actions is three years. If the Convention does not govern, the suit is not time-barred, but removal was improperly granted because the case does not present a federal question.

On appeal, appellants renew their claim that the Convention does not apply to BA's conduct in this situation, while BA again contends that the Convention does apply. In the alternative, BA suggests that the Federal Aviation Act, preempts any state law claims arising out of BA's provision of travel services.

I. WARSAW CONVENTION

A.

The Convention generally regulates international air carrier liability. In particular, the carrier is liable for "damage occasioned by delay in the transportation by air" (art. 19) which arises in "international transportation" deems transport "performed by several successive air carriers" as "one undivided transportation, if it has been regarded by the parties as a single operation." The parties agree that they viewed appellants' return trip as a single operation. Finally, article 30(2) provides that "the passenger or his representative can take action only against the carrier who performed the transportation during which the accident or delay occurred."

Appellants do not allege that BA was negligent in *issuing* the Air Mauritius portion of their tickets. The common thread in this dispute is the question of whether BA's conduct in *reconfirming* a flight reservation is the service of an "air carrier" in the course of performing a contract for international transportation by air. If so, the Convention governs and we must affirm. If that conduct is more properly analogized to the service of an independent ticketing agent who could be subject to a state law negligence claim, appellants can survive the limitations hurdle.

B.

BA relies on the Second Circuit's decision in *Reed v. Wiser*, and its progeny. *Reed* itself rejected an attempt to circumvent the Convention's liability limitations through suing airline *employees* rather than the carrier itself.

Subsequent cases have extended *Reed*'s rationale to airlines' *agents* acting in furtherance of the contract of carriage. As the district court noted, a number of these cases can be read to extend the Convention's scope only to those agents performing services that the carrier would otherwise be legally *required* to provide. However, other cases sweep more broadly, bringing under the Convention's umbrella all services provided "in furtherance of the contract of carriage."

The district court rejected appellants' reliance on *Kapar v. Kuwait Airways Corp. Kapar* held that a defendant airline, which had merely issued a ticket for a flight on another carrier, had acted as an agent only and not a "carrier," such that it was not subject to suit under the Warsaw Convention for damages sustained when the flight was hijacked. Appellants attempt to turn *Kapar*'s liability limitation shield into a sword, arguing that the relevant transportation here was to be provided by Air Mauritius and that BA was at most its sales agent and not a "carrier" in the context of appellants' delay. This distinction is unpersuasive, however, because it implies that BA would face different liability rules for the same injurious conduct solely on the basis of whether the same "undivided transportation" involved a second airline.

Far more powerful is appellants' argument that the cases upon which BA relies generally involved acts occurring "during" carriage. Here, by contrast, the alleged negligence did not occur during performance of the contract of carriage but rather days before, when BA mistakenly reconfirmed appellants' reservations on a nonexistent flight. Appellants' suggested approach has commonsense appeal. Their damages simply did not arise from a delay *in the transportation by air* for purposes of Articles 19 and 30(2).

BA also argues that because it often takes on the role of "air carrier," a holding that the Convention governs would best serve the treaty's goals of uniformity and certainty regarding liability arising out of international air transportation. However, exalting the corporate form in the manner BA suggests does not serve these goals; rather, airlines and independent contractors should receive the same protections for the same activities. Likewise, we will not attempt to create an artificial distinction between the services typically provided by "carriers" and those typically provided by "non-carriers," or to limit the Convention's protections to those services that airlines are required by law to perform.

We therefore hold that the Convention's statute of limitations applies only to actions for delays related to the *performance* of the international transportation. We reject an "in furtherance of the contract" test as too broad: "[T]he Convention does not apply to all claims of injuries suffered in conjunction with international air travel."

Washington state law therefore governs appellants' cause of action for BA's alleged negligence in its capacity as a ticketing agent acting before commencement of the journey. The district court erred in holding that the Convention's two-year statute of limitations applied and that appellants' action was time-barred as a result.

We emphasize that BA's liability here is based upon its negligent act of reconfirming appellants' reservations days before departure in a situation where the "carrier" no longer served the route in question. Once the passenger presents herself to the carrier or its agents as ready to begin the air journey, the Convention generally governs liability for delays in the carrier's performance, and its provisions apply until completion of disembarkation at the destination airport. We leave to future cases the determination of the Convention's scope with respect to operational actions (*e.g.*, maintenance and repair) or decisions (*e.g.*, changes in schedules and frequencies) necessarily occurring hours or days before departure.

II. FEDERAL PREEMPTION

BA also argues that the Federal Aviation Act ("FAA") preempts appellants' state law claim. The district court did not reach this argument. The FAA states in relevant part:

> [N]o State or political subdivision thereof and no interstate agency or other political agency of two or more States shall enact or enforce any law, rule, regulation, standard, or other provision having the force and effect of law relating to rates, routes, or services of any air carrier.

The leading case in the area is *Morales v. Trans World Airlines, Inc.,* which found that the FAA preempted the enforcement of a detailed set of airline fare advertising guidelines based on state consumer protection laws. The Court found that § 1305(a)(1) manifested a "broad pre-emptive purpose," and held that the guidelines "relat[ed] to" airline rates.

We hold that the FAA does not preempt appellants' state law negligence claim. In *Air Transport Ass'n of Am. v. Public Util. Comm.*, we suggested that the FAA did not preempt a California regulation banning the airlines' common practice of secretly taping calls to their reservations agents. We determined that the regulation generally prohibiting such taping did not "relate to" airline services, and emphasized that telephone reservations systems were not "peculiar to airlines."

Moreover, whereas *Morales* itself addressed a set of quasi-official guidelines addressing airline tariff advertising and *Air Transport Ass'n* involved a state agency's regulation, we recently interpreted *Morales* in a more analogous individual action in *West v. Northwest Airlines, Inc.* In *West*, plaintiff brought a claim for compensatory and punitive damages under state contract and tort law against defendant airline, which had bumped him from one of its flights. We held that it was unclear whether such claims fell within the FAA's "preemption reach." We then looked to FAA regulations, issued well before *Morales*, and noted that they gave the plaintiff the option of seeking a state court compensatory remedy. We concluded that the regulation remained a permissible construction of the statute, but that it did not contemplate punitive damages. We therefore held that the FAA permitted the state law compensatory claim. Since the general thrust of airline deregulation endorses competitive practices such as overbooking and Congress has effected airline deregulation through amendment of the FAA, however, we held that the FAA preempted the claim for punitive damages. *Id.*

Obviously, FAA regulations do not discuss remedies for negligent reconfirmations. However, appellants' case against preemption is even stronger than that in *West*. The conduct of which appellants complain in no way serves the goals of airline deregulation; permitting this state law cause of action to go forward has far "too tenuous, remote, or peripheral" an effect on air carrier services for the FAA to preempt it.

III. ATTORNEYS' FEES

Appellants have requested attorney's fees under 28 U.S.C. § 1447(c). However, "[a]n award of attorney's fees is inappropriate ... where the defendant's attempt to remove the action was fairly supportable and where there has been no showing of bad faith." This case does not support such an award.

REVERSED AND REMANDED.

[NOTE: Case citations and footnotes have been omitted.]

APPENDIX E

+ +

OUTSIDE THE CONVENTION

+ +

WOLGEL V. MEXICANA AIRLINES
821 F.2d 442 (7th Cir. 1987)

JOEL FLAUM, CIRCUIT JUDGE:

Joseph and Edythe Wolgel appeal from the dismissal of their claim for discriminatory "bumping" under § 404(b) of the Federal Aviation Act of 1958. The district court held that their claim was time-barred by the two-year statute of limitations contained in the Warsaw Convention. We reverse and remand for further proceedings.

I.

Because the Wolgels' complaint was dismissed for failure to state a claim under Federal Rule of Civil Procedure 12(b)(6), we must accept their factual allegations as true. According to their complaint, Mr. and Mrs. Wolgel arrived at O'Hare Airport on April 17, 1981, with two round-trip tickets that they had purchased from the defendant Mexicana Airlines for travel on that day from Chicago to Acapulco, Mexico. The Wolgels held confirmed reservations, and had complied with the relevant pre-boarding conditions. However, when the Wolgels presented their tickets and baggage to Mexicana's passenger agent, they were informed that no seats were available on their flight. In short, the Wolgels had been "bumped." The Wolgels assert that this incident occurred pursuant to a policy of substantial and consistent overbooking and overselling of confirmed reservation passenger seating.

The Wolgels submitted a claim for boarding compensation, as provided for by Civil Aeronautics Board regulations, but Mexicana refused to compensate them. Consequently, on April 17, 1986, exactly five years after their injury, the Wolgels filed suit in the Circuit Court of Cook County, alleging breach of contract, tortious breach of a contractual relationship between the parties, and discriminatory bumping (bumping in violation of Mexicana's own priority rules) in violation of § 404(b) of the Federal Aviation Act. On May 14, 1986, Mexicana removed the suit to federal district court pursuant to 28 U.S.C. § 1441, on the ground that Mexicana, a corporation wholly owned by the government of Mexico, is a foreign state within the meaning of the Foreign Sovereign Immunities Act. Mexicana then moved to dismiss the complaint on the ground that the Wolgels' action was time barred under the two-year statute of limitations contained in Article 29 of the Warsaw Convention ("the Convention"). The district court granted Mexicana's motion and dismissed the complaint. This appeal followed.

II.

The Wolgels base their federal claim on § 404(b) of the Federal Aviation Act ("FAA"). Section 404(b) prohibited domestic and foreign air carriers from subjecting any person to "any unjust discrimination or any undue or unreasonable prejudice or disadvantage in any respect whatsoever." In *Karp v. North Central Airlines,* this court held that § 404(b) created an implied private right of action for passengers of a domestic airline who were bumped due to a failure of the airline to follow its own boarding priority rules. However, neither in *Karp* nor in later cases did this court establish a statute of limitations for such actions. The Wolgels urge us to borrow the Illinois "catch-all" statute of limitations, which provides a five-year period in which to bring suit.

Mexicana Airlines argues, however, that the Warsaw Convention is the Wolgels' exclusive remedy. The Warsaw Convention is a multilateral treaty to which both the United States and Mexico are adherents. The Convention provides for uniform documentation for passengers and cargo on international flights, and limits the liability of air carriers in the event of accident or loss. The Convention also provides a remedy for claims of personal injury, loss of or damage to baggage, and delay. Actions based on the Convention must be brought within two years. The district court held that the Convention provided the Wolgels' only remedy. Because the Wolgels did not file suit until five years after their injury, the district court held that their claim was time-barred.

We conclude that the Wolgels' claim falls outside the Warsaw Convention, because the Wolgels seek damages for the bumping itself, rather than incidental damages due to their delay. Therefore, the two-year statute of limitations for claims covered by the Warsaw Convention does not apply to this case. Borrowing from the analogous state statute of limitations, we hold that the applicable statute of limitations for a claim of discriminatory bumping under the FAA is five years. Because the Wolgels' complaint was timely filed, we reverse the judgment of the district court and remand for further proceedings.

A.

Article 19 of the Warsaw Convention provides that "[t]he carrier shall be liable for damage occasioned by delay in the transportation by air of passengers, baggage, or goods." The first question in this case is whether this provision extends to claims of discriminatory bumping. We conclude that it does not.

"[T]reaties are construed more liberally than private agreements, and to ascertain their meaning we may look beyond the written words to the history of the treaty, the negotiations, and the practical construction adopted by the parties." The history of the Warsaw Convention indicates that the drafters of the Convention did not intend the word "delay" in Article 19 to extend to claims, such as the Wolgels', that arise from the total nonperformance of a contract.

The Second International Diplomatic Conference on Private Aeronautical Law was convened in Warsaw, Poland on October 4, 1929. On the Fourth day of the conference, the conference delegates discussed Article 21, the predecessor of Article 19. Mr. Ambrosini, the delegate from Italy, remarked that Article 21 did not provide a remedy for nonperformance:

For example, goods are delivered to the carrier: They are within the aerodrome, the aircraft did not leave, the contract is not performed. Must one say that the carrier is liable or not? Without doubt, he is, but it must be so said in the Convention, but Article 21 says nothing.

Mr. Ambrosini proposed that Article 21 be amended to provide for liability "in case of nonperformance of the contract, or of delay." However, after further discussion of this question, it became clear among the delegates that there was no need for a remedy in the Convention for total nonperformance of the contract, because in such a case the injured party has a remedy under the law of his or her home country. The delegates therefore agreed that the Convention should not apply to a case of nonperformance of a contract.

This case is one of nonperformance of a contract. The Wolgels are not attempting to recover for injuries caused by their delay in getting to Acapulco. Rather, their complaint is based on the fact that, as far as the record shows, they never left the airport. Because the Wolgels' claim is for total nonperformance of a contract, the Warsaw Convention is inapplicable.

The decision in *Mahaney v. Air France* supports our conclusion. In *Mahaney*, the plaintiff was bumped from a flight between New York and Puerto Vallarta, Mexico. Three years later, she sued the defendant under § 404(b) of the FAA. The defendant argued that the suit was barred by the two-year statute of limitations contained in Article 29 of the Warsaw Convention. The court held that the plaintiff's claim for the cost of renting a van—an incidental cost she incurred because of the delay—arose under the Convention. This claim was therefore time-barred. However, the rest of the plaintiff's claims were based on the discriminatory bumping itself, and the emotional harm caused by the bumping. The *Mahaney* court held that these claims did not arise under the Convention, because they did not stem from delay. Thus, the Convention's statute of limitations did not bar the remainder of the plaintiff's claims.

Mexicana relies on *Harpalani v. Air India*. In *Harpalani*, the plaintiffs, who were bumped from a flight between Bombay, India and New York, sued under Article 19 of the Warsaw Convention. The court held that the Warsaw Convention provided their exclusive cause of action, and dismissed the plaintiffs' other federal and state claims as "preempted" by the Convention. However, in reaching its conclusion the court did not examine the legislative history of the treaty, but simply relied on *Mahaney* and on *Hill v. United Airlines*. Neither case supports the proposition that Article 19 of the Convention provides a cause of action for bumping.

Finally, Mexicana's interpretation of the Warsaw Convention—that the Convention is the exclusive remedy for passengers bumped from international flights—rests on an anomalous reading of the FAA. Section 404(b) of the FAA prohibited discrimination by an "air carrier or foreign air carrier." Mexicana asks us to interpret the word "discrimination" to include discriminatory bumping when applied to domestic air carriers, but not when applied to foreign air carriers. We reject such an improbable reading of the FAA.

We conclude that the Warsaw Convention does not provide a cause of action for bumping. Therefore, the two-year statute of limitations set forth in Article 29(1) of the Convention does not bar the Wolgels' claim.

B.

We are left with the question of the applicable statute of limitations for claims brought under the FAA. We conclude that the appropriate limitations period is five years.

"When Congress has not established a time limitation for a federal cause of action, the settled practice has been to adopt a local time limitation as federal law if it is not inconsistent with federal law or policy to do so." Illinois provides a two-year statute of limitation for personal injury claims, a ten-year statute of limitation for contract claims, and a five-year statute of limitation for, among other things, "all civil actions not otherwise provided for."

Section 404(b) of the FAA is concerned with more than personal injury or breach of contract. The statute reflects "a desire to provide widescale protection against discriminatory rates and practices," and prohibits "unjust discrimination" in broad terms. The five-year period of limitations in ¶ 13-205 is thus the most appropriate state statute.

We adopt a five-year statute of limitations for claims brought under § 404(b). The Wolgels' complaint, which was filed exactly five years after their injury, is timely.

III.

The Wolgels' suit for discriminatory bumping under the FAA is not barred by the two-year statute of limitations set forth in the Warsaw Convention, because the Convention does not cover actions for bumping. Rather, the applicable statute of limitations for the Wolgels' FAA claim is a five-year period borrowed from Illinois law. Because the Wolgels filed their suit exactly five years after their injury, their complaint was timely. The judgment of the district court is reversed and the case remanded for further proceedings.

[NOTE: Case citations and footnotes have been omitted.]

APPENDIX F

+ + + + + + + + + + + + + + + + + + + +

ACCORD AND SATISFACTION

+ + + + + + + + + + + + + + + + + + + +

CURTIN V. UNITED AIRLINES, INC.
275 F.3d 88 (D.C. Cir. 2001)

MERRICK GARLAND, CIRCUIT JUDGE:

Three United Airlines passengers, on behalf of themselves and others similarly situated, sued United under an international treaty known as the Warsaw Convention to recover the value of baggage lost on international flights. Without reaching the question of class certification, the district court granted summary judgment against the three named plaintiffs, on the ground that each had entered into an accord and satisfaction with United by accepting a check from the air carrier "in full and complete settlement of any and all claims." We affirm the judgment of the district court.

I

In September 1998, James Curtin flew from Cork, Ireland to Dulles Airport in Virginia. After landing at Dulles, he reported that a bag of golf clubs, estimated to be worth $921, was missing. In January 1999, Margaret Wombacher flew from London to Chicago. One of her bags never arrived in Chicago, and she reported a loss of $1855. In the same month, David Simmons flew from London to Atlanta, connecting through Chicago. His bag made it to Chicago but not to Atlanta, and he filed a claim for $1355.

In response to the claims for compensation filed by Curtin and Wombacher, United sent each a letter stating:

> Because your itinerary involved an international destination, claim settlement is governed by the Warsaw Convention' which limits our liability to $635 due to loss, damage or delay.

It sent Simmons a slightly different letter, which read:

> As your trip involved international travel, payment for your loss is based on the weight of your checked bag. The maximum liability our company assumes is $9.07 per pound, up to 70 pounds per checked item unless excess valuation is declared and purchased prior to travel. Our check for $635 in settlement for the missing property, will be mailed to you shortly.

Subsequently, United mailed each plaintiff a check for $635. Above the endorsement line on each check was the following legend:

By endorsement of this check payee(s) agree that the amount shown is accepted in full and complete settlement of any and all claims which payee(s) may have against United Air Lines, Inc., its connecting carriers, their agents or employees for loss, damage or delay sustained by reason of an incident involving a United flight.

Curtin, Wombacher, and Simmons all signed and deposited their checks, the latter after consulting with an attorney.

Article 18 of the Warsaw Convention, an international air carriage treaty ratified by the United States in 1934, creates a cause of action against an air carrier for loss of or damage to a passenger's checked baggage. Article 22(2) of the Convention limits a carrier's liability for such loss to a maximum of 250 francs per kilogram, or $9.07 per pound. United calculated its liability to each plaintiff as no more than $635—the amount it tendered by check—because the maximum weight of a bag permitted on its flights was 70 pounds. Article 4(3) of the Convention, however, requires that baggage checks contain certain particulars, including the number and weight of the bags, and Article 4(4) states that "if the baggage check does not contain" those particulars "the carrier shall not be entitled to avail himself of those provisions of the convention which exclude or limit his liability." It is undisputed that United did not record the weight of any of the plaintiffs' bags.

In *Cruz v. American Airlines, Inc.*, this circuit ruled that the plain language of Article 4(4) precludes an air carrier's invocation of the liability limits of Article 22(2) when it has not recorded the weight of the baggage. *Cruz* acknowledged that passengers are not prejudiced by an airline's failure to note a bag's weight if the carrier's maximum weight allowance is used to determine the amount of its liability, and that in such circumstances the recording requirement "makes little real sense." Nonetheless, *Cruz* concluded that "the language of the Convention is unyielding and we have no warrant to dispense with portions we might think purposeless."

This case was filed on November 17, 1999, five weeks after the decision in *Cruz*. The First Amended Complaint was brought by Curtin, Wombacher, and Simmons, as a class action on behalf of themselves and all others similarly situated. The class was defined as all persons who checked baggage on an international United flight "without the weight of that baggage having been recorded," and who received payment of less than what they claimed was the fair value of the loss of or damage to that baggage—such payment "being an amount (usually $635) which United asserted or believed was the limit of its liability for such baggage loss/damage under Warsaw's Article 22(2) $9.07 per pound liability limitation." Plaintiffs proposed a class period "beginning the two years prior to initiation of this suit and ending on March 3, 1999." They claimed that they were entitled to recover the full value of their lost or damaged baggage, and that the Warsaw Convention's liability limit was inapplicable because the weight of their baggage had not been recorded on their baggage checks.

United moved for summary judgment pursuant to Federal Rule of Civil Procedure 56, raising the defense of accord and satisfaction by virtue of plaintiffs' endorsement and deposit of the checks that United had tendered in settlement of their claims. Plaintiffs countered that there were no valid accords and satisfactions, and that even if there were, they should be rescinded on the grounds of mistake and/or misrepresentation. Plaintiffs also asked the district court to permit discovery and to rule on the issue of class certification before addressing defendant's motion for summary judgment. The district court denied those requests and granted United's motion.

II

We begin with two preliminary matters: plaintiffs' contentions that the district court erred by deciding United's motion for summary judgment (1) without permitting discovery and (2) without ruling on the question of class certification. The first of these arguments is readily dispatched. Although it is true that summary judgment ordinarily "is proper only after the plaintiff has been given adequate time for discovery," plaintiffs' briefs fail to identify any facts essential to opposing United's motion as to which discovery is needed. Moreover, at oral argument, plaintiffs agreed that in light of factual concessions made by United below, all the facts required to decide the summary judgment issue are already in the record and further discovery is unnecessary. Accordingly, there is no possible ground for reversing the district court's denial of discovery.

The certification issue detains us only slightly longer. The plaintiffs assert that the district court was obliged to determine whether their suit could proceed as a class action before it could consider the merits of their individual claims, in light of Federal Rule of Civil Procedure 23(c) and the Supreme Court's holding in *Eisen v. Carlisle & Jacquelin*. Neither of these authorities, however, suggests that a court is barred from rendering an easy decision on an individual claim to avoid an unnecessary and harder decision on the propriety of certification.

We begin with Rule 23(c), which states only that the district court shall determine whether a case may be maintained as a class action "[a]s soon as practicable after the commencement of [the] action." As the Seventh Circuit has noted, although a certification decision will usually be "practicable" before the case is ripe for summary judgment, that will not always be so, and the word "'practicable' allows for wiggle room"—enough to make the order of disposition of motions for summary judgment and class certification a question of discretion for the trial court.

Nor is *Eisen* to the contrary. There, the Court reversed a district court that had held a preliminary hearing on the merits of the case in order to decide whether the plaintiff should be required to bear the cost of notice to the members of the asserted class. "We find nothing in either the language or history of Rule 23," the Court said, "that gives a court any authority to conduct a *preliminary inquiry* into the merits of a suit *in order to determine whether it may be maintained as a class action.*" Nothing of the sort occurred here. The district court did not conduct a preliminary inquiry, but rather reached a final resolution on summary judgment. Moreover, it did so to determine not whether the case could be maintained as a class action, but rather whether any of the named plaintiffs had a viable claim on the merits. Under such circumstances, nothing in *Eisen* or Rule 23(c) requires the district court to rule on class certification before granting or denying a motion for summary judgment.

As plaintiffs note, it is often more efficient and fairer to the parties to decide the class question first. But that was not so in this case where, as we discuss below, the district court readily and correctly perceived fatal flaws in plaintiffs' claims. Reversing the usual order of disposition in such circumstances spares both the parties and the court a needless, time-consuming inquiry into certification.

Plaintiffs also observe that it is often more protective of the interests of defendants to begin with the issue of class certification, because only a merits decision made after certification will bind all members of the class. But here, the defendant itself sought an early decision on the merits and, needless to say, does not suggest that it was prejudiced by winning on that basis. Nor do the named plaintiffs suggest any prejudice to their own interests traceable to the order in which the district court made its decision, rather than to the decision itself. The plaintiffs do contend that, due to the passage of time since the lawsuit began, when the suit is dismissed putative class members "will be left holding a time barred claim." That contention, however, is simply incorrect. The filing of a class action tolls the statute of limitations as to all asserted members of the class, and potential plaintiffs other than the three named in this case remain free to file their own suits against United. They will, of course, face the problem of stare decisis (at least in this circuit), but even so their legal position is better than it would be if the merits decision had been made after class certification— in which case they would face the bar of res judicata.

In sum, in circumstances like these, where the merits of the plaintiffs' claims can be readily resolved on summary judgment, where the defendant seeks an early disposition of those claims, and where the plaintiffs are not prejudiced thereby, a district court does not abuse its discretion by resolving the merits before considering the question of class certification.

III

We now turn to plaintiffs' challenge to the district court's grant of summary judgment in favor of United on the ground that plaintiffs' damage claims are barred by the doctrine of accord and satisfaction. We review the district court's decision to grant summary judgment de novo, and may affirm only if there is no genuine issue of material fact and the moving party is entitled to judgment as a matter of law.

Plaintiffs contend that (1) there were no valid accords and satisfactions in this case, and (2) even if there were, they should be rescinded on the grounds of mistake and/or misrepresentation. We consider each of these arguments below. Plaintiffs maintain that we should look to federal common law to decide these issues, while United urges us to look to the law of each individual passenger's domicile. That, however, is a dispute we need not resolve. Both sides agree that the Uniform Commercial Code (U.C.C.) and the Restatement (Second) of Contracts provide the applicable legal standards regardless of which law governs. And neither side cites any case to suggest that the choice of law would effect a difference in the interpretation of the relevant U.C.C. or Restatement provisions.

A

U.C.C. § 3-311 is entitled "Accord and Satisfaction by Use of Instrument." It provides, with exceptions not relevant here, that a claim is discharged if the person against whom the claim is asserted proves that: "(i) that person in good faith tendered an instrument to the claimant as full satisfaction of the claim, (ii) the amount of the claim was unliquidated or subject to a bona fide dispute, and (iii) the claimant obtained payment of the instrument." U.C.C. § 3-311(a). In addition, the instrument or an accompanying written communication must contain "a conspicuous statement to the effect that the instrument was tendered as full satisfaction of the claim."

The district court held that United's tender to each plaintiff of a check for $635, stamped with the legend that the payee's endorsement would constitute acceptance in "full and complete settlement of any and all claims which payee(s) may have against United Air Lines, Inc.," became an effective accord and satisfaction when the plaintiff signed and deposited the check. On appeal, plaintiffs' challenge relies only upon the second U.C.C. requirement: that the amount of the claim be unliquidated. The Restatement defines an "unliquidated" obligation as one "that is uncertain or disputed in amount." Plaintiffs contend that United's correspondence conceded the carrier's liability for $635, and thereby showed that United regarded each claim as an undisputed, "liquidated claim for $635."

At oral argument, plaintiffs agreed that, at least if considered in isolation, the legend stamped on United's checks indicated United's view that the amount in question was not undisputed, since it stated that endorsement would constitute "settlement" of all claims. Nonetheless, plaintiffs contend that the clarity of the

assert, did not demonstrate an intention to compromise or settle, but instead
flatly stated that United's liability was limited to $635—and thus rendered that
amount a liquidated claim.

This argument has two principal defects. First, the language of the letters
that United sent to the plaintiffs is not materially different from the language
on the checks. Like the checks, all three letters used the word "settlement" to
describe the nature of the transaction between the parties. Second, and more
important, there is simply no question but that the parties did consider the
amount of the claims to be in dispute, and hence that the $635 figure was far
from "liquidated." The three plaintiffs clearly did not regard $635 as the amount
they were owed, since their demands were for $921, $1855, and $1355. Nor did
United signal agreement that the amount it owed was in fact $635. Rather, the
carrier described $635 as the "limit" or "maximum" of its liability. That figure
was calculated solely on the basis of the maximum weight of plaintiffs' luggage,
and could have been reduced had United successfully challenged plaintiffs' esti-
mates of the value of the bags' contents.

There is only one way in which the $635 tendered by United could be con-
sidered evidence of a liquidated claim: if it were the law that a debtor automatically turns a debt (or a portion thereof) into a liquidated sum simply by
offering a fixed amount in settlement. But if that were the law, there would be
no such thing as an accord and satisfaction: every offer to settle a debt would
liquidate the debt (at least to the extent of the offer), rendering every such offer
ineligible under U.C.C. §3-311(a)(ii). In this case, in order to discharge a claim,
United paid more than it conceded owing and plaintiffs accepted less than they
conceded being owed. That is more than sufficient to satisfy U.C.C. § 3-311(a)
(ii), and the fact that the amount accepted was the same as the amount tendered
no more justifies calling plaintiffs' claims "liquidated" than it would those in
any other dispute. Accordingly, we conclude that the tender, endorsement, and
deposit of each check constituted a valid accord and satisfaction.

B

Finally, plaintiffs contend that, even if there were valid accords and satisfactions in this case, they should be rescinded on the grounds of mistake (unilateral or mutual) and/or misrepresentation. For either doctrine to apply in this
case, United's statements to plaintiffs must—at a minimum—have been "not
in accord with the facts." The point that was not in accord with the facts here,
plaintiffs contend, was United's claim that its maximum liability was limited
to $635, the product of $9.07 and the maximum weight of each plaintiff's

lost bag. Plaintiffs argue that, because the Warsaw Convention's liability limit applied only if United's baggage checks recorded the bags' actual weights, and because United's checks concededly did not do so, United's claim that there was any limit to its liability at all (other than the fair value of the lost baggage) was in error.

Had United's letters been sent or its checks tendered or deposited after this court's decision in *Cruz,* plaintiffs might have an argument for their position. But all of those events transpired months before *Cruz* was issued, and that subsequent decision can therefore play no role in the analysis. Instead, we must look to the state of the law at the time of the events in question. At that time, the applicability of Article 22(2)'s liability limit in the absence of the recording of weights required by Article 4 was an unsettled question, and the existing law provided a more than adequate basis for United to conclude that its view was correct.

When the accords and satisfactions in this case were reached, no Supreme Court or D.C. Circuit case had yet addressed the question subsequently decided in Cruz. The only federal appellate court to have considered the question, the Second Circuit, had held—consistent with United's view—that the liability limit of Article 22(2) continued to apply notwithstanding a failure to follow the requirements of Article 4. Two of the three state appellate courts to have ruled had also decided in accord with United's position. So, too, had many federal district judges, including all that had ruled in this circuit, although district courts had ruled the other way as well. Moreover, the position expressed in United's letters was supported by advice to passengers published by the United States Department of Transportation.

The plaintiffs have cited no authority, in any jurisdiction, suggesting that when an issue of law is unsettled, a party makes a misrepresentation or mistake by reaching a conclusion that is well supported by existing law. Measuring United's statement against the state of the law at the relevant time, we reject plaintiffs' contention that the accords and satisfactions are void for misrepresentation or mistake.

IV

We find no abuse of discretion in the district court's decision to rule on United's motion for summary judgment without first permitting discovery or ruling on class certification. Nor do we discern any error in the district court's grant of summary judgment in United's favor. Accordingly, the judgment of the district court is

Affirmed.

[NOTE: Case citations and footnotes have been omitted.]

TIMELINE OF COMMERCIAL AVIATION

1908 First passenger flight (conducted by Wilbur Wright)

1910 First commercial flight school (founded by Orville Wright)

1914 First scheduled passenger airline service (operated between St. Petersburg and Tampa)

1919 KLM begins operations (the oldest carrier in the world still operating under its original name)

1920 Minneapolis-St.Paul International Airport opens for commercial service

1921 First in-flight movie (on Aeromarine Airways)

1923 First transcontinental nonstop flight

1924 Delta Air Lines founded

1926 United Airlines founded

1926 Congress passes Air Commerce Act, which authorizes Secretary of Commerce to designate air routes and license pilots

1926 First flight lands into Candler Field (now Hartsfield-Jackson Atlanta International Airport), the busiest airport in the U.S.

1930 First female flight attendant hired by Boeing Air Transport (now United Airlines)

1933 United Airlines begins flying coast to coast

1935 Boeing designs first commercial aircraft with pressurized cabin

1935 Amelia Earhart dedicates North America's first commercial airline terminal (at Newark)

1936 Pan American begins passenger flights across the Pacific Ocean

1939 Pan American begins transatlantic passenger service

1939 New York Municipal Airport opens and is later renamed LaGuardia Airport after the city's mayor

1958 Federal Aviation Act passed by Congress

1959 American Airlines offers first domestic jetliner flights with routes from New York to Los Angeles

1967 Federal Aviation Administration is established

1971 Southwest Airlines begins service, with Dallas to Houston as its only route

1972 Delta Air Lines purchases Northeast Airlines

1973 The first female airline pilot, Emily Warner, flies for Frontier Airlines

1976 Concorde jet completes first supersonic passenger flight

1978 Airline Deregulation Act is enacted

1979 First frequent-flier program

1981 11,400 air traffic controllers are fired by President Reagan

1982 Braniff International files for bankruptcy

1986 Northwest Orient purchases Republic Airlines and changes name to Northwest Airlines

1987 Frontier Airlines, New York Air, and People Express merge into Continental Airlines

1991 Eastern Airlines and Pan American Airways cease operation

1993 First ticketless travel becomes available

1995 First airline tickets sold via the Internet

1997 ValuJet Airways merges into AirWays Corp. and becomes AirTran Airways

1998 Smoking is banned on all domestic flights

1999 First web-based passenger check-in and online boarding passes

2001 American Airlines merges with Trans World Airlines

2001 Transportation Security Administration established in response to September 11 attacks

2004 World's longest commercial flight begins (19 hours and 9,534 miles on Singapore Airlines flight from New Jersey to Singapore)

2007 Airbus A380 (capable of carrying 850 passengers) introduced

2008 Delta Air Lines merges with Northwest Airlines

2009 Transportation Security Administration adopts scanners as primary method of pre-flight screening

2010 Southwest Airlines acquires AirTran

2011 Airbus announces 200 planes ordered by AirAsia, largest contract in airline history

2012 United Airlines merges with Continental Airlines

2013 American Airlines merges with US Airways

ABOUT THE AUTHOR

Cecil C. Kuhne III is a litigator in the Dallas office of Fulbright & Jaworski L.L.P. As a former travel writer who has logged a lot of miles on airplanes, he loves to fly. It's just that he loves *not* to fly even more.